Prescription For Murder

A thriller

Norman Robbins

GW00566713

Samuel French — London
www.samuelfrench-london.co.uk

ISBN 978 0 573 11338 3

CHARACTERS

Barbara Forth, 30s
Dr Richard Forth, Barbara's husband, mid 50s
Dorothy Livingstone, 45
Mary Haigh, late 60s
Allan Haigh, Mary's husband, late 60s
Eric Dawson, computer salesman, 40s
Julia Moore, Richard's ex-girlfriend, about 45

SYNOPSIS OF SCENES

The action takes place in the living-room of the Forths' detatched house in Bere Knighton, north Devon.

ACT I
SCENE 1 Friday afternoon
SCENE 2 The following Saturday. Early evening

ACT II
SCENE 1 The following Wednesday. Early afternoon
SCENE 2 The following Friday morning

Time — the present

COPYRIGHT INFORMATION

(See also page ii)

Other plays and pantomimes by
Norman Robbins
published by Samuel French Ltd

At the Sign of "The Crippled Harlequin"
Aladdin
Ali Baba and the Forty Thieves
Babes in the Wood
Cinderella
Dick Whittington
The Grand Old Duke of York
Hansel and Gretel
Hickory Dickory Dock
Humpty Dumpty
Jack and Jill
Jack and the Beanstalk
The Late Mrs Early
Nightmare
Pull the Other One
Puss in Boots
Red Riding Hood
Rumpelstiltzkin
Sing a Song of Sixpence
Slaughterhouse
Sleeping Beauty
Snow White
Tiptoe Through the Tombstones
Tom, the Piper's Son
Tomb with a View
Wedding of the Year
The White Cat
The Wonderful Story of Mother Goose

For Gaye and Jeremy Salter
for coffee and biscuits,
and "Twiggy" for occasional breakfasts

ACT I
Scene 1

The living-room of the Forths' detached house in Bere Knighton, north Devon. Friday afternoon

It is a gracefully proportioned room, typical of mid-Victorian buildings, and decorated with taste. French windows occupy a large area of the wall UC, *giving access to a paved patio with floral tubs and a view of the garden. Rich drapes, neatly swagged, hang at each side of the windows. To the* R *of the windows stands a large, glass-fronted bookcase, crammed with assorted hardback books of varying age.* L *of the windows there is a well-stocked drinks table on which there are assorted glasses*

R, *an Adam-style fireplace is sandwiched between two tall recessed windows through which mature trees and shrubs can be glimpsed. Matching swagged drapes hang and bowls of fresh flowers occupy the deep ledges. Beneath each window is a built-in unit. The upstage unit supports a music centre and speakers, with a sizeable collection of classical records and CDs on the shelving below. The* DS *unit supports a television set, and on the shelving below there is a VCR recorder and assorted video tapes. Assorted ornaments stand on the mantel of the fireplace, with two large oriental vases occupying the outer edges and a valuable looking clock placed in the centre. A large mirror hangs above the fireplace*

A half-round table stands DL *on which there is an attractive modern lamp.* UL *there is a small writing desk and ladder-back chair occupying the space immediately below a door. Writing paper, envelopes, pens, etc. are in, or on, the desk, together with framed photographs.* US *of the door, which opens on to the desk and leads to a hall and the rest of the house, there is another bookcase. This is open-fronted and filled with paperbacks and less imposing volumes. Just in front of the french windows, facing front but angled slightly towards the fireplace, is a large comfortable settee.* R *of the settee is a small occasional table.* L *of the settee is a matching easy chair angled towards the television. Cushions are on the settee and the easy chair. The room is thickly carpeted and decorative plates and pictures fill the wall space. There is a light switch* L *of the door*

The two windows R *are open, as are the french windows. On the patio, Dorothy Livingstone, a cheery middle-aged woman in a smock, is vigorously shaking a small, shaggy rug. A vacuum cleaner stands at the side of the settee, its lead snaking across the floor to a hidden powerplug. Dusters, spray polish cans and window cleaners are on the settee and a pair of rubber gloves are on the settee arm*

Barbara Forth, an attractive woman in her thirties, enters through the doorway L. *She wears a pastel boiler suit and carries two mugs of coffee. She sees Dorothy and reacts*

Barbara (*plaintively*) Not there, Dorothy. It'll all be back in the room.
Dorothy (*cheerfully shaking her head*) No, it won't, Mrs Forth. Wind's blowing in the other direction. (*She gives her hair a flick then enters the living-room. Indicating the mug*) I'll just put this down then we can move into the dining-room. (*She moves over to the fireplace*)
Barbara (*surprised*) You've not finished already? (*She holds out a mug*) I haven't been gone five minutes.
Dorothy (*placing the rug on the hearth*) Doesn't take me long when I set my mind to it. I can go through this place like a dose of salts, as my Grandma Eccles used to say. (*She straightens herself and takes the proffered mug*) Ooh, lovely. I'm just about ready for this. (*She smiles and sips her drink*)
Barbara (*jokingly*) And what about the bookcase? (*Indicating the glass-fronted bookcase*) You haven't done that?
Dorothy (*firmly*) I certainly *have*. It's been polished from top to bottom.
Barbara And the books? You've taken all those out?
Dorothy (*raising her eyebrows*) Didn't see the point. You're not likely to get dust behind *them*, are you? They're squashed in like sardines.
Barbara (*smiling*) Which is exactly why I want them doing. Lord knows what's lurking behind those cracked cardboard covers. I bet they haven't been touched since he moved in. And you know how long ago *that* was. (*She sips at her coffee*)
Dorothy (*searching her memory*) Six years come August, I think. Same as Mr Linney at the hardware shop.
Barbara (*justified*) Yes. So we'll have them all out and see if we can't put them back again in some sort of order. (*She sips again*)
Dorothy (*doubtfully*) Well, if you say so. But I don't expect he'll be too pleased about it. You know what he's like about having his things moved. I remember the fuss he made when you brought that big jardiniére thing downstairs, last year. It had to go back on the landing, didn't it? (*She sips her coffee*)

Barbara That was different. And anyway, we're not *moving* them, are we? Just tidying them up. He probably won't even notice. I don't think he's laid a finger on them since we were married. They just sit there gathering dust and glowering at me. (*She sips at her coffee*)

Dorothy (*putting her mug on the mantle and sighing*) We'd best make a start then. Do you want them on the floor or shall I stack them on the settee?

Barbara Definitely on the floor. Then while I'm sorting them out, you can ——

The front doorbell chimes

(*Pulling a face*) That's all we need. Visitors.

Dorothy Do you want me to go?

Barbara (*shaking her head*) I'll do it. It's probably for Richard anyway.

Barbara puts her mug on the desk and exits L

Dorothy moves up to the bookcase, opens it, and begins lifting the books from the shelves, stacking them haphazardly on the floor

There is the sound of voices in greeting off stage

(*Off*) Come in. Come in. Go through.

Mary enters L, followed by her husband, Allan. Both are in their late sixties and look fit and healthy. Mary wears a skirt and blouse, sensible shoes and carries a handbag. Allan wears white trousers, a sleeveless sweater, shirt and shoes, and carries a battered leather bowls bag

Mary (*noticing Dorothy; beaming*) Someone looks busy.

Dorothy (*agreeably*) No rest for the wicked. Hello, Mary, Allan.

Dorothy returns to the books

Barbara enters L, behind them

Mary (*facing Barbara*) We've not caught you at a bad moment, have we?

Barbara (*quickly*) No, no. Just a bit of spring cleaning — three months too late. Dorothy's giving me a hand so I can get it done before Richard's back from Barnstaple.

Allan You're feeling better, then?

Barbara (*with feeling*) You've no idea. But the rest must have done me good. I haven't had so much energy in months. (*Suddenly*) Would you like a cup of something? I've only just boiled the kettle.

Mary No, thank you. We had one in the pavilion before we came away. At least, I did. (*She glances at Allan*) He was drinking shandy.

Allan (*beaming*) We were playing Fremington in the quarter final.

Barbara So I heard.

Barbara plucks dusters and her cleaning things from the settee

A good match, was it?

Allan Depends on your viewpoint. They beat us by three points. Mind you, we didn't have Cliff Berry on account of his being on holiday with their ——

Mary (*pleasantly interrupting him*) Allan. Give it a rest, can't you? Not everybody's bowls-mad like you. (*She chuckles*) Wind him up and he'll go on for hours. I know *I* have to put up with it, but there's no need for him to inflict it on *you*. (*Seriously*) Now, we've not come to disturb you. It's just that we were passing by and I thought we'd drop in and see how you were feeling. I never expected to find you on your feet — let alone doing housework.

Barbara (*dismissively*) It was nothing serious. Just a stomach bug. A few days in bed and I'm as good as new again.

Barbara indicates for them to sit on the settee and Allan moves towards it

Allan Well, that's something to be grateful for. We thought it might have been more of that trouble you had at Christmas. (*He sits and puts his bag between his feet*)

Barbara (*hastily*) Heaven forbid. I wouldn't want to go through that again. (*She laughs*) I really thought I was dying.

Mary They never *did* find out what it was, did they?

Barbara (*wryly*) No. But I'd rather not be reminded, thank you. Too many unpleasant memories.

Barbara deposits the cleaning things on the bookcase L

Dorothy (*turning*) It really makes you think, though, doesn't it? They can give you a new heart and kidneys, but half the time they haven't a clue what's going on in your innards. (*To Mary*) Remember old Mrs Wells in Fore Street?

Mary (*hastily*) Yes. But I'm sure Barbara doesn't want to hear about *that*, Dorothy. The poor woman's been gone ten years. (*To Barbara; confidentially*) One of the previous doctor's patients. Used to keep her gallstones in a glass jar on the dresser and wave them in your face when you visited. Quite proud of them, she was. (*She smiles*) Anyway, as long as we know you're all right.

Barbara (*brightly*) Yes. Yes. I'm fine. It was good of you to call.

Mary (*firmly*) We'd better be off, then. Come on, Allan.

Mary moves to leave

Allan (*surprised*) Eh? (*Realizing*) Oh. (*He picks up his bag and rises*) Bye, Barbara. Dorothy.

Mary (*opening the door*) We'll see you next week.

Barbara (*suddenly remembering*) Oh. I haven't paid you, have I? For the tickets. Or have you seen Richard?

Mary (*shaking her head*) There's no hurry. You can give it to me later. (*She smiles*) I don't imagine you'll be running away.

Barbara No, but you'd better have it now while I remember. If you hold on a minute, I'll just get my purse.

Barbara hurries past Mary and exits

Mary (*half-heartedly*) It doesn't matter. (*To no-one in particular*) There was no need. It would have done next week.

Allan (*to Dorothy*) I bet Richard's pleased she's up and about again. He was getting quite worried about her.

Dorothy Yes. But I wouldn't believe everything she tells you, if I were you. She's not half as well as she makes out. Just putting a brave face on things, if you ask my opinion.

The others stare at Dorothy

If it were anything to do with me, she'd have stayed in bed 'til the end of the week. Why he didn't take her to hospital, I'll never know. It's not normal to be having the pain she's been having and I don't care what anybody says.

Allan (*awkwardly*) Well, I'm sure he would have done if he'd thought it were necessary. He's a good enough doctor.

Mary (*nodding*) Excellent.

Dorothy I wouldn't know. I've never been ill in my life. But I must say he didn't seem half as worried about her as I was. He was out for half the day and most the night, Monday and Tuesday.

Mary (*defensively*) He has got the practice to run.

Dorothy I'm not saying he hasn't. But you didn't see her Tuesday afternoon. She was so bad about three, I had to phone the surgery and leave a message for him to come home. And when he did make an appearance, he as much as told her she was making a fuss about nothing. She was in tears after he'd gone again.

Mary (*frowning*) That doesn't sound like Richard.

Dorothy (*drily*) Well, maybe you've got to live with them to find out what they're really like.

Barbara pops her head round the door

Barbara Must have left it upstairs. I won't keep you.

Barbara vanishes from sight again

Mary (*turning to speak to Barbara*) It doesn't … (*She realizes Barbara has gone and turns back to Dorothy*) Well, she seems to have made a speedy enough recovery, doesn't she? (*Kindly*) Let's hope it's all behind her, now. (*Changing the subject*) Will you and Colin be coming on Wednesday? They've still a few tickets left.

Dorothy I don't think so. It's not really our cup of tea. And he doesn't finish work 'til seven, so it'd be a bit of a rush, in any case.

Allan Well, if you happen to change your minds …

There is a chime from the main door which startles everyone

Dorothy (*frowning*) I'll just see who that is.

Dorothy exits L

(*Off; calling out*) I'll get it.

Mary (*to Allan; softly*) I can't understand that, can you? About his not being worried. He seemed quite concerned when I saw him at the Guild meeting.

Allan (*shaking his head*) You can't go on what Dorothy says. Nine times out of ten she gets the wrong end of the stick. I know she means well, but the man *is* a doctor. He'd know if there were something really wrong with her. And obviously there wasn't. Just some sort of enteritis. We've all had it from time to time, haven't we?

Mary (*frowning*) She does seem to have had a lot of stomach trouble since they got married, though, doesn't she? I wonder if it's the water? You know how poorly you were that time in Spain.

Allan There's nothing wrong with the water 'round here. It's the best in Britain.
Mary (*drily*) And the most expensive. But all the same ...

Dorothy enters, followed by Eric. He is an attractive man in his early forties, smartly dressed in a lightweight suit. He has a slightly embarrassed look on his face

Dorothy A visitor for Mrs Forth.

The trio smile shyly at each other

(*To Eric*) She'll be down in a minute.
Eric (*hesitantly*) I'm not interrupting, am I? I mean ——
Mary (*quickly*) No, no. We're just about ready for leaving. We only dropped in to see if she was feeling any better. (*She smiles at him*)
Eric (*frowning*) Is she not well, then?
Dorothy She's back on her feet again, if that's anything to go by, but she only got out of bed yesterday.
Eric Nothing serious, I hope?
Allan (*smiling*) Not this time. Just a bit of tummy trouble.

Allan pats his stomach and Mary throws him a disapproving glance

Dorothy (*curiously*) She's not expecting you, is she? I mean, she didn't say.
Eric (*quickly*) Oh, no. No. She's not. (*He grins shyly*) In fact, I'm probably the last person she'll be expecting.

The others look at him questioningly

We, er, well — we were engaged at one time. (*Embarrassed*) It didn't work out. There was a business problem and I had to go to Canada for a couple of years. When I got back, I found she'd left town to marry Dr Forth and moved to this end of the country. (*Hastily*) There were no hard feelings between us, and as I've got a job on in Ilfracombe at the minute, I thought I'd drive over and say hello again. Maybe treat them to a meal as a belated wedding present, or something. (*He smiles nervously*)
Dorothy (*not knowing what to say*) Fancy.
Mary Well, I'm sure she'll be glad to see you.
Allan Could be just the tonic she needs.

Barbara enters, hurriedly, clutching her purse and a ten pound note

Barbara Found it on top of the linen basket. I can't think *what* I was doing with it in *there*. (*She presses the money into Mary's hand then turns to Eric with an apologetic smile*) Sorry to have kept you. I was just paying my debts.

Eric looks at Barbara blankly then looks at the others

(*Puzzled*) Is something wrong?
Eric (*hesitantly*) Mrs Forth?
Barbara (*brightly*) Yes.
Eric (*confused*) I'm awfully sorry. I seem to have made a mistake. You'll have to forgive me.
Dorothy (*to Barbara*) Don't you know him, then?
Barbara (*blankly*) Should I?
Eric (*stricken*) This is so embarrassing. I, er, I thought you were some-one else. A girl I knew in Derbyshire.

Barbara looks at the others in bewilderment

I *do* apologize. It was just that the name was Forth. They said he lived in this part of the world so I assumed I'd got the right one. He's the only Dr Forth I could trace. I can't tell you how sorry I am.
Barbara (*baffled*) It might help if I knew what you were talking about.
Allan He said you were engaged to him, one time.

Barbara looks at Eric in astonishment

Eric (*helplessly*) I feel such an idiot. It's all a stupid mistake on my part. I was engaged to a girl in Buxton, you see — Grace Walker. Her father was a local businessman. Absolutely rolling in it. But he didn't exactly approve of me. Thought I was after her money to prop up my own business, which was going through a pretty rough patch at the time. To cut a long story short, we agreed to break things off and I went to Montreal to see if I could drum up business over there. When I got back, old Walker had died and a neighbour told me Grace had left town to marry a doctor she'd met at some resort in Italy. Apparently they were living in this area. As I was down here on business, I did a bit of asking around and thought I'd drop in for a surprise visit. (*He grins wryly*) The only trouble is, I seem to have got the wrong people.
Barbara (*sympathetically*) Well, there's no harm done. It was a genuine mistake.
Eric It was Mrs *Richard Forth*, I was looking for.

Barbara (*smiling*) Well, he's certainly called Richard, but he's not the one you want, I'm afraid. I doubt he's been to Buxton in his life. And I know *I* haven't. (*Kindly*) Still, there's no harm done. Why don't you contact the BMA? I'm sure they'd be able to help you trace this other Dr Forth. There can't be *that* many of them practising in Devon. (*She smiles*) Richard'll be tickled pink when I tell him.

Eric (*awkwardly*) I wish you wouldn't. My face is red enough as it is. The less people who know about it, the better. (*Uneasily*) I'd better be going.

Barbara (*smiling*) I'll see you out. (*Kindly*) And don't worry. We all make mistakes.

Barbara exits into the hall

Eric gives an embarrassed smile to the others and exits into the hall. The door closes behind him

The trio look at each other solemnly for a moment, then chuckle in amusement

Dorothy Well. Who'd have believed *that* if you'd told them it down at *The Fox and Grapes*?

Mary Poor fellow. He must feel terrible. (*She chuckles*)

Allan Mind you, you can understand how it happened, can't you? The names being the same and everything. I remember a few years back we had a chap named Johnson down at the club and he marked his woods with a big letter I.

Mary All right, Allan. We don't want to know about it.

Allan (*insisting*) But the same thing happened to him. One of the other fellows ——

Mary It wasn't the same thing at all. That was just a mix-up. Now hush your noise and let's get going. If Ken and Valerie are coming round tonight, I want to give the room a going over before they arrive. The first thing she'll do when she walks in is run her finger over the sideboard looking for dust.

Dorothy Which is nothing to what his lordship's going to do if he walks in and sees his precious books strewn all over the carpet. You'll hear him screaming down at *The Butter Cross*.

Mary (*hastily*) Well, we won't hold you up any longer. And if you do change your mind about Wednesday …

Mary and Allan exit L

Dorothy turns back to the bookcase and finishes removing the books.
Depositing the last of them on the floor, she gets a duster and can of polish
from the desk top and attacks the shelves, grimacing at the grime

Dorothy (*to herself*) I don't know about six years' dust. It's more like
six *hundred*. Makes you wonder where it comes from.

Barbara enters, L

Barbara (*amused*) How about that for a novel way of livening up a
Friday afternoon? (*She crosses over to Dorothy*) I shall die if it turns
out to be a new kind of sales pitch for Paradine Computers.

Barbara drops to her knees and picks up a book from the stacks

Dorothy (*still polishing*) Who?
Barbara The firm he runs. He gave me one of his cards. (*She fishes the
card out from her pocket and reads it aloud*) Eric Dawson. Paradine
Computers, Station Street, Buxton. (*She puts the card back into her
pocket*)
Dorothy (*turning to her*) What makes you think it might be a sales
pitch?
Barbara Well, he didn't say as much, but he did mention that if Richard
was interested in a new system we could contact him. He's staying at
the *Starcross Hotel* in Ilfracombe for the next two days. Pass me one
of those dusters, will you?

Dorothy crosses to the desk

Dorothy So what about that story he was telling us? You don't think
he was making it up, do you? (*She sorts out a duster and hands it to
Barbara*)
Barbara I don't know what to think, to tell you the truth. (*Wiping the
book cover*) He certainly seemed embarrassed enough about it. It's
just the idea of two doctors with the same name practising in this part
of Devon that makes the mind boggle. I can't wait to see what Richard
makes of it. (*She examines the book*) You know, I don't think this has
ever been opened. It's in mint condition.
Dorothy (*frowning*) I don't suppose there's any chance he *hadn't* made
a mistake, is there?
Barbara (*looking up*) Sorry?
Dorothy (*turning back to the bookcase*) Well, you haven't been married
all that long, have you? I mean, maybe this is something that happened
before you came along, so to speak.

Barbara (*amused*) I can assure you Richard wasn't married to any Grace Walker before he met me. He was a widower, yes, but his first wife's name was Nancy. (*Handing the book to Dorothy*) Top shelf, I think.

Dorothy But she died about fifteen years ago, didn't she? Accident in the Lake District, or something? (*She puts the book on the shelf*) You'd not get *me* in a rowing boat if I couldn't swim a stroke. Especially one that hasn't been used in years. It's a wonder he didn't drown as well.

Barbara (*mildly*) If he'd been in the boat with her, he might have done.

Dorothy looks at her in surprise

It was her idea to take off alone. Richard hadn't a clue where she'd gone 'til they found the body. It must have been awful for him. Knowing he'd been sitting there reading, while she was in the middle of the lake fighting for her life.

Dorothy (*stunned*) He's never told us that. Oh, the poor love. No wonder he's so grumpy. (*Returning to her idea*) But what I'm meaning is, he'd only been living down here a few years before he met you, so maybe this "Grace" woman was somebody he knew before he moved here?

Barbara I shouldn't think so. (*She picks up another book*) When he swept me off my feet, he said I was the second great love of his life, and I'm sure if he'd been considering marriage with someone in between times, he'd have told me about it before today. (*She wipes the book*)

Dorothy (*holding out her hand for the book*) I wouldn't be too sure about that, if I were you. In my experience, men tell you what they want to tell you and that's as much as they want you to know. I was married to my Colin seven years before I found out he'd once spent a night in jail for being drunk and disorderly — and I hadn't even known he was a drinker.

Barbara (*handing her the book*) Top shelf again. (*She selects another book*) Well, I don't think there's any dark and dirty deeds lurking in Richard's background. He's just a common, old, boring country doctor with a gruff exterior and a heart of gold. (*She dusts the book*)

Dorothy (*drily*) You didn't think that on Tuesday afternoon when he had you in tears. (*She puts the book away*)

Barbara (*embarrassed*) Oh, I was just being stupid. You know how it is when you're feeling low. (*She hands her the book*) It doesn't take much to set the waterworks going. And he was perfectly right, wasn't he? Look at me now. Not a care in the world. (*She picks up another book*)

Dorothy Well, far be it from *me* to criticize.

The front doorbell chimes

I'll get it.

Dorothy puts the book on the shelf, drops her duster and exits L

Barbara continues dusting books and replacing them in the bookcase until Dorothy enters, tight-lipped, followed by Julia. She is a very smartly dressed woman of forty-five or so, not unattractive but rather cool and superior in manner. She carries a handbag

(*Disapprovingly*) Mrs Moore. (*She moves to bookcase and retrieves her duster*)

Barbara (*scrambling to her feet*) Hello, Julia. Excuse the mess. Just tidying up this ghastly bookcase. (*She indicates it loosely and grins*)

Julia (*haughtily*) So I notice. But please, don't let me disturb you. I just need the teensiest moment of Richard's time. Is he around?

Barbara (*apologetically*) I'm sorry. He's over in Barnstaple. At a meeting.

Julia (*frowning*) But he's expecting me. To collect the photographs.

Barbara Sorry?

Julia My passport photographs. He promised to countersign them.

Barbara Oh.

Julia And I *do* need them today.

Barbara (*biting her lip*) He must have forgotten. (*Hastily*) I mean — he didn't mention anything. (*Helpfully*) I could look in his study, if you like?

Julia (*tightly*) That would be helpful.

Barbara (*nodding*) Right. (*Indicating the settee*) Well, have a seat.

Barbara throws a helpless look at Dorothy and exits

Dorothy ignores Julia and begins polishing again

Julia (*after a pause*) Still charring, I see?

Dorothy (*flatly*) It's an honest enough job. (*She rubs at a stubborn spot*)

Julia I wasn't suggesting otherwise. (*She moves to the settee and seats herself*) Though it wouldn't appeal to me. Grubbing around in other people's dirt. (*She smiles sweetly and smoothes her skirt*)

Dorothy (*pausing in her work and turning*) That does surprise me, Julia. I always thought other people's dirt was exactly what appealed to you.

Julia (*frowning*) I'm sorry? (*She looks over her shoulder*)

Dorothy You spend so much time digging for it, it's a wonder you don't keep a shovel in your handbag.

Julia (*smiling and facing front again*) There's nothing wrong with healthy curiosity, Dorothy. In my opinion, apathy's far more reprehensible.

Dorothy is uncertain what the final word means and does not know what to say. Julia glances around the room

I thought Barbara might have done something with this by now. It's over a year since she moved in. I must say, it wouldn't suit me to have someone else's décor staring me in the face every day.

Dorothy (*tartly*) It's a good job you don't live here, then, isn't it? Because they seem to like it exactly the way it is. (*She turns back to her polishing*)

Julia Of course, Richard's totally oblivious to his surroundings, but I expected more of Barbara. From the way he extolled her virtues, I imagined a cross between Helen of Troy and Florence Nightingale. It came as quite a shock to find out she was just an ordinary mortal like the rest of us.

Dorothy Oh, I wouldn't describe you as ordinary, Julia. Not by a long chalk. And if you think Dr Forth's oblivious to his surroundings, then perhaps you don't know him as well as you think you do.

Julia (*amused*) Really? Well you might be surprised to find out just how well I do know him. (*Smugly*) If the lovely Barbara hadn't suddenly appeared on the scene, I could well have been occupying this house instead of Elm Cottage.

Dorothy (*easily*) Yes. I did hear you'd set your sights on him at one time. Quite a few people passed comment on it.

Julia (*sharply*) Oh?

Dorothy They were rather tickled when he upped and married somebody else.

Julia Small things amuse small minds.

Dorothy (*maliciously*) I hadn't realized it was a small thing, Julia. From the stories *I* heard, it seemed to be quite a *big* thing. You were so put out about it, you had to go away for weeks to get over the disappointment.

Julia (*feigning amusement*) Where on earth did you hear that? The reason I left Bere Knighton was to spend a fortnight on a Health Farm in Surrey followed by a few weeks in Scotland with friends. All arranged and paid for months before Richard sprang his unexpected re-marriage on everyone.

Dorothy And you never threatened to kill him for making a fool of you?

Julia (*laughing incredulously*) Certainly not.

Dorothy (*unconvinced*) Strange how many people must have suffered hallucinations that afternoon. At least a dozen of them thought you said the marriage wouldn't last six months.

Julia (*coolly*) I may have expressed a certain amount of surprise. I won't deny it. He'd hardly known her a month and there he was proposing to spend the rest of his life with her. But the poor man was at perfect liberty to marry anyone he chose. And in case the town gossips missed it, I was the first to congratulate them on their return from Switzerland.

Barbara enters L

Barbara (*apologetically*) I'm sorry, Julia. I can't find them anywhere. But he shouldn't be late back. Could you call again in an hour or so?

Julia (*rising; slightly peeved*) I don't seem to have much choice, do I? I need them this afternoon and I've a dinner engagement in Somerset tonight so I have to get my hair done.

Barbara (*helpfully*) I'll bring them 'round myself, then. As soon as he arrives. (*Cheerfully*) So, where are you heading? Switzerland, is it?

Julia (*blankly*) Switzerland?

Barbara I heard you mention it as I came in.

Julia Oh. (*Recovering*) Yes. Yes. A little place on Lake Lucerne.

Barbara (*smiling*) We stayed in Belalp — near the Aletsch Glacier. (*Dreamily*) It was absolutely wonderful. I never wanted to leave it. (*She smiles*) In fact I almost *didn't*. (*She laughs*) I went for a walk one afternoon while Richard went to the bank, and almost got flattened by a loose boulder that came hurtling out of nowhere. How it missed me I'll never know. I was still in shock when they found me. I can laugh at it now, of course, but at the time … (*She shakes her head*)

Julia (*staring at her*) He never mentioned *that*.

Barbara (*easily*) Oh, it was just one of those stupid things that happen now and then. It didn't spoil our honeymoon — but it certainly put a stop to my walking around on my own. (*She laughs*)

Julia (*with a glacial smile*) Well, I'd better be off. But if you'd remind him about my photographs, I'd be very grateful. As I said, time is getting short. (*She moves towards the door*)

Barbara Don't worry. I'll bring them round as soon as he gets back. (*She begins to follow her*)

Julia It's all right. I can see myself out.

Julia exits L

Dorothy (*glaring after her*) If ever a woman got up my nose, it's *that* one.

Barbara silently shushes her and closes the door

Barbara (*in a low voice*) I must admit she's not my favourite lady in Bere Knighton. (*Moving back to the books*) Whatever happened to Mr M? Does anybody know? (*She sinks to her knees again*)
Dorothy (*picking up a book to dust*) Haven't a clue. She left here to marry him about eighteen years ago, then came back the year before Dr Forth arrived, claiming to be a widow. She bought Elm Cottage from Mr Petheridge after his wife died. Lives with his daughter on Lower Road, now. Next door but one to the Methodist Church. (*She scours the book briskly*)
Barbara It's certainly a lovely house.
Dorothy They can all be lovely if you spend enough money on them. And heaven knows, she's not exactly down to her last million.
Barbara (*laughing*) Oh, come on, Dorothy. She's not worth that much. (*She gets a book*)
Dorothy I bet she's got more tucked away than you have. (*She puts the book in the case*)
Barbara (*amused*) That wouldn't take much doing. Richard's the moneyed one in this household. (*She dusts the book*) I'm only worth something when I'm dead.
Dorothy Same here. Eighteen thousand pounds my Colin would get if anything happened to me. And if it were the other way round, I'd only get twelve. It's no wonder they say it's a man's world. (*She picks up another book and glances at the title*) Karma Sutra? I didn't know doctors read books like this.
Barbara (*gravely*) Oh, yes. It's required reading for all doctors. Then when patients come complaining about sprained backs and things, they've got a good idea of what most of them have been up to.
Dorothy (*disbelieving*) Go on.
Richard (*off*) Anybody home?

They both react

Barbara (*startled*) Richard. (*She scrambles to her feet*)
Richard (*off*) Barbara?

The door opens and Richard Forth enters. He is an attractive man in his mid fifties with greying hair and a small moustache. He wears a lightweight three-piece suit and carries a slim attaché case. He reacts at the sight of the books

(*Sharply*) What are you doing?

Barbara (*moving towards him*) Spring cleaning.

Barbara attempts to embrace him, but he brushes her aside

Richard But these are *my* books. (*He puts his case on the desk, almost knocking over the coffee mug*) What are they doing all over the floor?

Barbara (*reasonably*) They had to come out so we could dust behind them.

Richard (*fuming*) There was no need to dust behind them. They were perfectly fine the way they were. How many times must I tell you, I don't like my things being moved? (*He crosses her, kneels and picks up a book*)

Barbara (*soothingly*) I know. I know. But the shelves did need doing, whether you think they did or they didn't. We could have grown tomatoes in the dust behind this lot, (*to Dorothy*) couldn't we, Dorothy?

Dorothy smiles wanly

Richard (*glaring at Barbara*) Don't be facetious, Barbara. Most of these books are first editions. Absolutely priceless. Careless handling could make them worthless.

Barbara (*kneeling beside him*) But we weren't handling them carelessly, darling. We were treating them like delicate pieces of Dresden.

Richard (*sharply*) You don't leave Dresden lying around on the floor.

Barbara (*contrite*) No, dear. I'm sorry. But if it hadn't been for a string of unexpected visitors, we'd have had them all back on the shelves before you arrived home and you wouldn't have known a thing about it.

Richard (*still fuming*) I can't understand this constant urge to change things around. Every time I walk in you're moving *something*. A chair, a desk, an ornament. I sometimes wonder if I'm in the right house.

Barbara *Now* who's being facetious? (*She kisses him lightly*) Welcome home.

Richard (*grumpily*) I'll give you a hand to put them away.

Barbara (*rising*) You'll do nothing of the kind. You'll go straight into your study and find those passport photographs you promised to sign for Julia Moore. She's just been round to collect them and wasn't very pleased when I couldn't oblige.

Richard *(groaning)* Oh, damn. *(He rises)* I did tell her to call for them this afternoon, didn't I? I think I took them to the surgery.

Barbara *(taking the book off him)* Well you'd better make sure, hadn't you? Because I promised to drop them in for her as soon as you arrived back.

Richard *(sighing)* It doesn't matter. I'll do it myself. Who else has been?

Barbara Mary and Allan Haigh. Just to see how I was. The little Cartwright girl, to ask if you could call in and see her mother before you started surgery tonight. She's still having some bleeding, apparently. And the computer man from Buxton who thought you'd married his ex-fiancée.

Richard *(frowning)* What?

Barbara *(grinning)* About half an hour ago. I was looking for my purse when he arrived and Dorothy let him in. He thought you'd married his ex-fiancée, Grace Watkins.

Dorothy *(chipping in)* Walker.

Barbara *(correcting herself)* Walker. *(To Richard)* And dropped in to say hello to you both.

Richard *(baffled)* Grace Walker? I've never heard of her.

Barbara That's what I told him. *(She smiles)* He was so embarrassed when he realized his mistake, he couldn't leave fast enough.

Richard *(frowning)* Did he say what his name was?

Barbara *(nodding)* Dawson. Eric Dawson. *(She gets the business card out)* He gave me his card.

Richard *(reading it)* Paradine Computers, Buxton.

Barbara *(lightly)* If you need a new system for the surgery, he'll be only too happy to speak to you. He's at the *Starcross Hotel* in Ilfracombe 'til Sunday.

Richard *(frowning)* And what made him think I knew this "Walker" woman?

Barbara I'll tell you later. It's not important. It was either a genuine mistake or he thinks he's found a new way to sell his computers. You go find those photographs while we finish off the room.

Richard I'd better give him a ring and find out what this is about.

Barbara Well, you can't do it now, He won't be back there, yet. Now shoo. Madame wants her photographs.

Richard Is there any chance of a cup of tea? My throat's as dry as a rasp.

Barbara I'll bring it through to you.

Dorothy *(quickly)* I'll put the kettle on, shall I? (*She stuffs her duster in her pocket*)

Barbara Make enough for all of us, will you? I never got the chance to finish the last one.

Dorothy collects the two mugs and exits

Richard *(awkwardly)* Oh — by the way, there's a chance I'll be going up to London for a while. Something cropped up at the meeting which might need dealing with urgently. If I do have to get a locum in, we'll need to put him up here again. That won't be a problem, will it?

Barbara No. We've plenty of bedrooms. But ——

Richard It'll only be a week, at most. Damned inconvenient, but if I don't keep on top of it, we're going to be in Queer Street. (*Briskly*) I'll find those photographs. (*He picks up his case*) And *do* get those books off the floor.

Richard exits

Barbara stands there motionless, a slight frown on her face. After a moment, she quickly dusts the book she is holding and replaces it on the shelf. Kneeling again, she continues to inspect, dust and case the remaining volumes

Dorothy enters

Dorothy Be ready in a couple of minutes. (*She crosses to the vacuum cleaner*) I'll put this back where it belongs, shall I? Or would you like me to give the dining-room a going over?

Barbara I think we'll tackle that tomorrow, if you don't mind. I'll finish putting these away and we can call it a day. I can feel my energy flagging by leaps and bounds.

Dorothy *(winding up the cable)* I'm not surprised. It's a wonder you've lasted the way you have. I'd have a nice hot bath, if I were you, then get your feet up for a while when you've had dinner. There's no point in doing too much and making yourself ill again. (*She picks up the vacuum cleaner and heads for the door*) You'll not get any thanks for it if you do, and that's a fact.

Dorothy exits

Barbara smiles and continues dusting books

Dorothy enters and begins collecting up dusters and polishes, etc.

Well, we've broken the back of it, anyway. There's only next door and the hall to do, and then we can start on the upstairs. You still want to do that, don't you?

Barbara (*quickly*) Oh, yes. I can't leave the place half done. Especially if Richard does go away and the locum stays here. Must try to give a good impression. (*She picks up another book and dusts it*)

Dorothy Another of his conferences, is it?

Barbara (*shrugging*) Suppose so. We didn't really discuss it. It's nothing definite, in any case. But if it does happen, I'll have to think of something for him to do at nights. He won't want to sit here with me, watching television. Let's hope he'll like a drink and I can pack him off to *The Fox and Grapes* for an hour or two.

Dorothy You could always throw a pile of books into his lap and let him get on with them.

Barbara (*reading the title of the book she is holding*) Yes. *Psychomotor Epileptic Seizures: Their Causes and Treatment*. That should keep him interested for a day or two.

Barbara idly flicks open the book and looks at the flyleaf. A strange expression appears on her face and she looks up at Dorothy

Dorothy Something wrong? (*Anxiously*) You're not feeling ill again?

Barbara (*shaking her head; oddly*) This inscription.

Dorothy (*puzzled*) What about it?

Barbara (*reading aloud*) To my darling, darling Richard. All my love, Grace.

The two women look at each other silently as the Lights fade

SCENE 2

The same. Early Saturday evening

The room has been tidied, the fire lit, and the windows closed. Darkness is falling and the main lights are on. Julia, expensively swathed, sits on the settee, a glass of brandy in her hand. Her handbag is on the desk. Richard, coatless, stands at the french windows, gazing into the darkening garden and clutching a tumbler of whisky

Julia (*after a pause*) I don't know what to say, Richard. It's the most extraordinary thing I've ever heard. Are you sure you haven't seen it before?

Richard (*sharply*) Of course I'm sure. Do you think I don't know what's in my own bookcase?

Julia But the inscription?

Richard (*turning to her*) Doesn't mean a thing to me. Not a single damned thing.

Julia And she doesn't believe you?

Richard Can you blame her? First this — this *idiot* tells her he thought I'd married his ex-girlfriend, and not an hour later she finds a book in my bookcase with the bloody woman's name written in it. No wonder she's behaving as though I'm a latter day Dr Crippen.

Richard moves DR

Julia (*soothingly*) I'm sure it's not that bad, darling.

Richard (*bitterly*) Isn't it? (*He drains his glass*) I should never have married her. She's neurotic, suspicious, and a total hypochondriac. I sometimes wish she *would* kill herself and get it over with.

Julia (*surprised*) Richard.

Richard (*shaking his head*) I'm sorry. I shouldn't have said that. It's just … Oh, what's the use? (*He gazes into his glass*)

Julia (*rising and moving to him*) What did you mean? You sometimes wished she would kill herself? She hasn't made threats, has she?

Richard Forget it.

Julia (*insistently*) But I want to know, Richard. Has she?

Richard (*grudgingly*) Once or twice. Half a dozen times, I suppose.

Julia But why? For what reason?

Richard (*bitterly*) Headaches. Cramps. Nausea. Cost of living. Price of jam. You name it and *she*'ll have a reason. (*He moves towards the drinks table*)

Julia And what exactly's wrong with her?

Richard (*snapping*) Nothing's wrong with her. Not a single damned thing. She'll outlive the rest of us. (*He pours himself a refill*)

Julia (*reasonably*) She has had more than her fair share of illness these past few months.

Richard (*moving to the easy chair*) I've had Norton at Birchester General take a look at her. Prendergast at Moorfield Infirmary, Plumley from Invercote, and even Collins at the Westminster. They've all come to the same conclusion. If there is anything wrong with her, it's purely psychosomatic. (*He drinks*)

Julia Then shouldn't she be seeing someone?

Richard (*irritated*) Of course she should. I've argued 'til I'm blue in the face but she won't damn well listen. (*He sits*) Look. Can we drop this? I shouldn't have brought it up in the first place. It's not something I need to discuss right now.

Julia But you do, Richard. (*She moves to his side and perches on the arm of the chair*) I've a vested interest. Remember? (*She puts her arm around his shoulder*)

Richard touches Julia's hand and sighs deeply

Richard I should have spotted it right away. This passion for high drama. Always needing to be the centre of attraction. I'm supposed to be a doctor, for God's sake. (*He drinks*)

Julia (*soothingly*) You are, darling. And a very good one. Far better than this place deserves.

Richard (*bitterly*) Not that anyone else has noticed. As far as they're concerned, there'll never be another doctor like (*mockingly*) dear Dr Bradley. "*He* never needed blood samples and skin scrapings, et cetera. *He* knew exactly what was wrong with me — just by looking." (*He drains his glass*)

Julia (*briskly*) Bradley was a fool. In a perfect world he'd have been struck off years before he retired. He tried telling me I was too reliant on sleeping tablets and didn't really need them. I was so furious I reported him to the medical council. (*She notices Richard's glass is empty*) Can I get you another?

Richard (*glancing at his watch*) Better not. She'll be back, shortly.

Julia (*standing*) In that case, I'll make myself scarce. (*She drains her glass*) Mustn't let the green-eyed monster add to your troubles, must we?

Richard (*fervently*) Oh, Julia. Why didn't I marry you when I had the chance?

Julia (*shrugging*) You met Barbara.

Richard (*bitterly*) Yes. I met Barbara. (*He stares into his glass*)

Julia (*pointedly*) But I'm still available. If you want me.

Richard (*startled*) You mean … ?

Julia (*quickly*) Oh, no. Not as a mistress. (*She smiles*) I'm very possessive, Richard. I couldn't possibly share you. I'd want you all to myself.

Richard (*ruefully*) In that case, it's out of the question. Divorce isn't an option. Not for good Catholics.

Julia (*smiling*) Pity. But at least you *know*. (*Briskly*) Right. I'd better be off. I'm dining with the Metcalfs at eight. They've offered to keep an eye on things whilst I'm away so I could hardly wriggle out of it.

Thank God we're going to the *Charterhouse* and not having one of her
famous casseroles. I swear she got the recipe from the Borgias.

Richard (*rising*) I'll drive you down there.

Julia (*raising an eyebrow*) Do you think that's wise?

Richard To be honest, I don't really care. (*He takes her glass*) I'll just
give these a rinse and get the coats.

Richard exits

*Julia smiles in satisfaction before moving to the mirror and gazing into
it*

Julia (*thoughtfully*) So. We've been talking suicide, have we? How
very … interesting.

*Julia moves to the desk and opens her handbag. Fumbling inside it, she
produces her compact and lipstick and proceeds to repair her flawless
features*

*After a moment, Richard enters. He is wearing his jacket and carries
her coat*

Richard One coat, milady. And your carriage awaits.

Julia (*archly*) Why, thank you, Jeeves.

*She replaces the compact and lipstick, closes the bag, then slips into the
coat with his assistance*

(*Fastening the buttons*) I've just been thinking.

Richard Yes?

Julia About this book business.

Richard (*tiredly*) Julia.

Julia (*facing him*) No, Richard. Listen to me. Isn't it possible it was put
there by this Dawson fellow?

Richard (*shaking his head*) I spoke to the Haighs last night. They
seemed to think he was genuine. Swore blind he'd nothing in his
hands when he came in and never went near the bookcase.

Julia Did you ring the hotel he was staying at?

Richard (*tartly*) Of course I did. I'm not an idiot. (*Calming slightly*)
He hadn't arrived back and they'd no idea how late he'd be. It was
half past ten the night before. I was going to ring again, but some idiot
called me out to an accident, Combe Martin way, and I spent half an
hour or so driving round back lanes in torrential rain looking for a

non-existent farm before finding out the whole thing was a hoax. What with that and running a bloody badger down on the A39, by the time I got back here I was seething. The last thing I had on my mind at that time was chasing him up.

Julia (*sympathetically*) I'm not surprised. But you've tried again? Surely?

Richard (*nodding*) Before surgery, this morning. But he'd checked out last night. As soon as he arrived back.

Julia (*frowning*) That's a little unusual, isn't it?

Richard (*scornfully*) Apparently he'd met someone who desperately needed his services and offered to put him up while they worked out the details. (*Pointedly*) But don't worry. I'll be ringing his office in Buxton first thing Monday morning. I'm going to get to the bottom of this if it's the last thing I do.

Julia You'll let me know what happens?

Richard (*nodding*) You can count on it.

Julia picks up her bag and turns to exit

(*Suddenly*) Julia?

Julia turns to him

Thanks for coming 'round this evening. It's really appreciated. Made a welcome change from twenty-four hours of hurt looks, pursed lips and clattering saucepans.

Julia smiles and turns back to the door. As she does so, voices are heard from the passageway

Barbara (*off*) I can manage it now, thanks. It was just with the key in my hand.

Allan (*off*) It's no trouble. We're not in any hurry.

Julia glances quickly at Richard

Mary (*off; impatiently*) Wipe your feet, Allan. You're not at home now.

Barbara (*off*) Go on through. I'll just put these in the kitchen and get the kettle on.

The door opens and Allan enters. He stops short when he sees Julia and Richard

Mary (*off*) Go on.

Mary pushes Allan into the room and enters behind him

Richard (*forcing a smile*) Allan. Mary. Come in.
Mary (*beaming*) Hello, Julia. We've not seen you for a while. Still keeping well, I hope?
Julia (*coolly*) Yes, thank you.
Allan (*anxiously*) We're not intruding, are we?
Richard (*easily*) Not a bit of it. We were just leaving. I'm heading for the surgery and I said I'd drop Julia at the Metcalfs.
Mary (*dismayed*) You've not been called out on a Saturday night? (*Indignantly*) Honestly. Some people.
Richard (*cutting in*) No, no. It's nothing like that, Mary. I just need the notes on the Eastment boy again.
Mary (*sympathetically*) Oh, the poor little soul. I heard about it from Mrs Parkin at the W.I. It doesn't seem fair, does it? A child that age. (*Anxiously*) He's going to get better, though, isn't he? He will recover?
Richard We certainly hope so.
Mary (*to Julia*) It'll break his mother's heart if anything happens to him. It's only a year since she lost Derek. (*Sighing*) It always happens to the nice ones, doesn't it?
Allan (*to Richard; proudly*) We won the Guineaford match this afternoon.
Mary (*heavily*) Allan. The only one interested in that is you. There's more to life than bowling, you know. (*She shakes her head and sighs*)
Richard (*amused*) It's all right, Mary. (*To Allan*) You can tell me about it when I get back. I shouldn't be more than fifteen minutes.
Allan Well, not if you're not interested.
Mary (*reprovingly*) Oh, don't start getting sulky, Allan. He's already told you. (*To Julia*) They're all the same, aren't they? Just like children. Tell them they can't do something and out comes the bottom lip. (*She rolls her eyes*) Men.
Richard (*moving behind her to the door*) I'll see you later.
Julia (*following Richard*) Good-night.
Allan 'Night.
Mary 'Night.

Richard and Julia exit and the door closes

(*To Allan*) Well don't stand there making the room look untidy. Sit yourself down. (*She begins to unfasten her coat*)

Allan (*moving to the settee*) There was no need for that, you know. I was only making conversation. (*He sits*)

Mary (*removing her coat*) Perhaps you were — but you do go on about it. You're as bad as Alice Timmins with her gardening. Anybody'd think no-one ever grew a dahlia before she came along. (*She puts her coat on the settee back*) Now old Mrs Philbeam was what I'd call a gardener. I've never seen ——

The door opens and Barbara enters

Barbara Was that the door?

Mary (*turning to her*) Julia Moore and Richard. He's dropping her off at the Metcalfs on his way to the surgery.

Barbara Oh. (*She glances at the door*)

Mary (*moving to sit next to Allan*) But he won't be long. About fifteen minutes, he said.

Barbara (*hesitantly*) And, how did he seem? I mean …

Mary (*brightly*) Fine. As far as I could see. What did you think, Allan?

Allan Well …

Mary (*ignoring him*) Just his normal self. (*Kindly*) Now stop worrying about it. There'll be a perfectly good explanation, you mark my words.

Barbara (*helplessly*) But he lied to me — and it's all so stupid. I mean, I'm not the jealous type. He's an attractive man. There's bound to have been other women between Nancy dying and me coming along. I accept that. So why won't he admit that he knew her?

Allan Maybe he feels embarrassed about it? If they were going to get married and something went wrong at the last minute, well, he might prefer to forget it ever happened, mightn't he?

Barbara (*moving R; bewildered*) But the look on his face when I showed him the book. I thought he was going to faint.

Mary (*shaking her head*) It seems so out of character.

Barbara (*miserably*) I know. And that's what's worrying me. I always thought he'd tell the truth if it killed him, but after this …

Allan (*uncomfortable*) Yes. Well.

Barbara (*bitterly*) It was there. (*Indicating the bookcase*) In that bookcase. It's absolutely ridiculous of him to say he's never seen it before. And every time I raise the subject, he flies off the handle or walks out of the room. (*She dabs at her eyes*) I don't know if I can take any more of it.

Barbara moves to the windows and draws the curtains

Mary (*throwing a quick glance at Allan*) It can't be as bad as that, m'dear.

Barbara (*moving behind the easy chair*) But it is. He's changed. Suddenly it's like living with a stranger. We can't even talk to each other. (*She forces a smile*) Perhaps it's partly my fault? I've not been on sparkling form these past few months and even the smallest things are getting me down. Everything's such an effort.

Mary (*kindly*) I know how you feel. I was just the same before they found out about my thyroid. All I wanted to do was sleep. (*Thoughtfully*) I suppose you've been tested for that, haven't you? Thyroid problems?

Barbara (*dejectedly*) I think I've been tested for everything. But according to Richard there's not a thing wrong with me. He thinks it's psychosomatic.

Mary (*surprised*) You mean — you're *imagining* it? (*Concerned*) That's ridiculous, Barbara. *Everybody* knows how ill you've been. He can't be serious?

Barbara (*smiling wanly*) I don't know. Perhaps he's right. But if it is psychosomatic, why is it happening to me? I was fine yesterday. Well, up to the argument about the book. After that I just had to go upstairs and lie down. I hadn't eaten a thing, but I can't begin to tell you how sick I was. I only just made it to the bathroom. Dorothy was here another hour trying to calm me down. (*She sits on the arm of the easy chair*)

Allan (*sagely*) Nervous stomach, by the sound of it. Our Irene ——

Mary (*cutting in*) And what was Richard doing?

Barbara (*slightly embarrassed*) He'd had to go out. There was an emergency call from somewhere Combe Martin way that turned out to be a hoax. He was absolutely livid when he got back here.

Allan I'm not surprised. They ought to have more sense, these young hooligans. I know what I'd do with them.

Barbara Anyway, he made me a hot drink and insisted I stayed in bed, but half an hour later I was ill again. And the pain. It was like a knife cutting into me. I spent the rest of the night hoping to die and Richard moved into the spare bedroom to try and get some sleep.

Mary (*concerned*) Oh, Barbara, love. You should be seeing a specialist.

Barbara I have done. Several of them. But they say there's nothing wrong with me.

Mary (*firmly*) Then in my opinion they're not doing their jobs. (*Pointedly*) And I'm surprised at Richard for not taking it any further.

Barbara (*defending him*) He did put me on a fresh course of tablets last week. I've got to be fair to him. But until we see how they effect me, there's nothing to do but wait. (*Ruefully*) The only trouble is, this book business has made everything so unpleasant between us. I'm not sure they're doing any good.

Allan (*hesitantly*) Well, I can't help thinking you might be making a mountain out of a molehill.

Mary glances at him sharply

I mean, I know you found that inscription, but what makes you think it was written by this Walker woman?

Barbara (*looking at him strangely*) Because she's signed it.

Allan No, no. You said it was signed *Grace*. Not Grace *Walker*. Just Grace.

Barbara (*not following his reasoning*) So?

Allan So couldn't it have been signed by somebody else called Grace?

Mary (*impatiently*) Well, of course it couldn't, you great booby.

Barbara (*shaking her head*) He told me it wasn't his book. He'd never seen it before.

Mary (*glaring at Allan*) And if it isn't his book, what was it doing in his bookcase? It didn't jump in there by itself.

Allan (*patiently*) I'm not saying it did. I'm just raising possibilities.

Mary Well don't bother yourself.

Allan (*persisting*) Perhaps somebody else put it there?

Mary (*scornfully*) Like who, for instance? Father Christmas?

Allan Well — one of the locums. There's been a dozen or so to my recollection. And most of 'em have stayed here while he's been away. Maybe one of them was called Richard?

Mary (*despairingly*) Oh, Allan.

Barbara (*hopefully*) I could easily find out. There's a list in his study.

Mary (*pleading*) Barbara.

Barbara (*standing*) It won't take a minute. And I'll get that tea while I'm at it.

Barbara exits

Mary (*glowering at Allan*) Allan Haigh. Will you ever learn to keep your big mouth closed?

Allan (*surprised*) What have I said now?

Mary You and your might's and maybe's. Of course there hasn't been a locum here called Richard. You've raised her hopes and now they're going to be shattered again. With friends like you around, she certainly doesn't need enemies.

Allan How do *you* know what the locums were called? They were all "Doctor" to us?

Mary Well, they didn't call the last two Richard, did they? They were both women.

Allan sighs and rolls his eyes

And it's no use rolling your eyes. She's going to come back in here feeling ten times worse than she was when she went out. And it'll all be your fault.

Allan (*protesting*) I was only trying to help.

Mary Yes. Well you'd help a lot more if you kept your nose out of it and let me look after things.

Allan Why? What are you going to do?

Mary (*firmly*) We've known Richard a long time. Almost six years. And I think we can call him more of a friend than just the local doctor. I'll have a quiet word with him about what's going on and we'll see if we can't get to the bottom of it. (*She frowns*) He must know who Grace Walker is. And whatever the reason he's pretending he doesn't, he's got to see what this is doing to his marriage. We can't let things go on the way they are going. Not if we still want to consider ourselves his friends.

Allan (*sighing*) Have it your own way, then. But I'm not sure he'll appreciate it.

Barbara enters, smiling happily, an open desk diary in her hand

Barbara (*relieved*) You were right, Allan. It's here on his list. Look. (*She leans over the settee to show them*) Richard C. Ellis. Five days in June and a fortnight in October. Four years ago.

Allan (*triumphantly*) There you are. What did I tell you?

Mary (*to Allan; with chagrin*) Looks like someone owes someone else an apology.

Barbara (*happily*) I can't believe it. All that anguish for nothing. If only I'd thought of it earlier.

Allan (*smugly*) Just needed a touch of genius, that's all.

Mary (*pushing him*) Oh, go on with you.

Barbara I'll get the tea.

The doorbell chimes

(*Rolling her eyes*) I'll just get that.

Barbara exits, carrying the diary

Mary I knew there had to be an explanation. It was so out of character.

(*Resignedly*) I expect you'll be crowing about this from now to Christmas.

Allan (*easily*) Well, it's time I had some credit for a bit of sense. The way you go on …

Barbara (*off; surprised*) Mr Dawson.

Mary and Allan turn their heads to the door in surprise

Eric (*off*) I'm sorry to trouble you again …

Barbara (*off*) No. No. Not at all. Come in.

Eric (*off*) You're sure you don't mind?

Barbara (*off*) Is something wrong?

Eric (*off*) No, no. I mean — it's nothing medical. Just chasing up a lost pen.

Barbara (*off*) Pen?

Barbara enters, followed by a pale looking Eric

Eric A gold Sheaffer. With a maple leaf engraved on the barrel. I thought I might have dropped it here. (*He sees Mary and Allan*) Oh, hello again.

They exchange smiles

(*To Barbara*) It's got great sentimental value and I can't find it anywhere. (*He looks at her hopefully*)

Barbara (*shaking her head*) I haven't seen one. Are you sure you had it here?

Eric Well, I think I did, but I can't swear to it. I mean, I wrote down a few addresses during the afternoon, but it was missing when I got back to the hotel. I'd hate to have lost it.

Barbara (*thoughtfully*) I could give Dorothy a call. She might have seen it and put it somewhere safe. (*Deciding*) Have a chair. I'll call her as soon as I've brought the tea in. You will have a cup with us?

Eric (*awkwardly*) It's very kind of you, but …

Barbara Sit over here.

She takes Eric's arm to direct him to the easy chair. He gasps in pain, jerking his arm away and clutching it

(*Confused*) I'm sorry. (*She looks at him anxiously*)

Eric (*forcing a smile*) It's all right. Just a bit tender. I had an accident last night. Nothing broken, thank goodness. Just bruises and sore muscles.

Barbara (*uncertainly*) I see.

Eric (*ruefully*) Apart from clinching a major deal, it hasn't been too brilliant a week for me. First, I make a fool of myself by coming here yesterday. Then I lose my pen and almost landed in hospital through not looking where I was going. (*He grins*) I'm lucky to escape so lightly.

Mary What happened?

Eric (*dismissively*) Just my own stupid fault. After I'd eaten last night I went for a walk round the town. I could have sworn the road was clear before I stepped off the pavement, but suddenly this car came out of nowhere and headed straight for me. There was no way it could have stopped, so I threw myself sideways between a couple of parked vans and it shot past me doing at least sixty. By the time I got to my feet again, it was out of sight.

Mary (*shocked*) That's terrible.

Barbara Didn't anyone get the number?

Eric There was no-one else around.

Allan But you reported it to the police?

Eric As soon as I'd stopped shaking. Though I'm not expecting it to do any good. Probably a joyriding drunk or a doped-to-the-eyeballs teenager. And I only got a glimpse of what it looked like. A dark blue or black Volvo. How many of those things are running around these days?

Allan That's right. (*To Barbara*) You've got one yourself, haven't you, Barbara? A black Volvo. (*Hastily*) Not that I'm saying it was yours.

Mary (*glaring at him*) I should hope not.

Allan I just meant it's a popular make.

Eric Anyway, I told them what I could and they said they'd look into it, but I suppose it's the last I'll hear of it.

Barbara The trouble is, even if they do catch somebody, they'll probably get off with a warning or be sent on holiday by the Social Services. It really makes you wonder what the world's coming to, doesn't it? (*She gives a quick smile*) I'll get that tea.

Barbara exits

Eric moves hesitantly to the chair and sits

Mary (*confidentially*) I always use witch hazel to bring bruises out. I expect it's a bit old fashioned for you younger folks, but it does work, you know. Just dab it on with a bit of cotton wool and you'll feel the difference in minutes. You can get it at most chemists.

Allan (*helpfully*) Arnica or something, they call it these days.

Eric (*giving a tight smile*) Thanks.

Mary I can't believe no-one came to help you.

Eric (*wryly*) It's always the way, isn't it? A main road on a Friday night and not another soul in view.

The door opens and Richard enters

Richard (*heartily*) Quicker than I thought I'd be. Lights were with me for a change.

Richard sees Eric and looks questioningly at the others

Eric (*rising*) Dr Forth, is it? Eric Dawson, Paradine Computers. (*He holds out his hand*)

Richard (*ignoring it*) Dawson?

Eric (*awkwardly*) I, er, called yesterday afternoon.

Richard (*realizing*) You mean you're the idiot who told my wife this cock and bull story about Grace Wilson?

Eric Walker, actually. But …

Richard (*furiously*) Wilson. Walker. What the hell's it matter? If you've come here to cause trouble, you'll find you've bitten off more than you can chew. (*He crosses to the bookcase and opens it*) Now take your bloody book and clear off (*He snatches the book out and thrusts it at Eric*) And if I catch you round here again, I'll call the police. Is that understood?

Eric (*baffled*) I think you're making a mistake.

Richard I'm not making anything. Now get out before I throw you out.

Allan (*attempting to rise*) Just a minute, Richard ——

Richard (*snapping*) Stay out of it, Allan.

Allan But ——

Eric I don't know what you're talking about. That isn't mine.

Richard You brought it here.

Eric I've never seen it before.

Richard (*flipping open the book cover*) Are you denying that this is your girlfriend's writing? (*He thrusts the book at Eric again*)

Eric (*glancing at it*) I wouldn't know. Look ——

Mary (*to Richard; soothingly*) Richard, dear. Just let me say something.

Richard The only thing I want to hear, Mary, is what the hell he's playing at.

Barbara enters with a tray on which she carries four teacups and saucers, a teapot, a sugar bowl, two small milk jugs, three teaspoons and a small plate of assorted biscuits

Barbara (*taking in the scene*) Richard.

Richard (*glaring at her*) And what's he been telling you this time? That I'm really Jack the Ripper?

Barbara (*putting the tray on the desk*) Of course he hasn't. (*She hurries to him*) Oh, Richard. It was my fault. I jumped to conclusions exactly the way you're doing now. Mr Dawson's got nothing to do with it. Honestly.

Richard Then what's he doing here?

Eric I came to see if I'd left my fountain pen. Mrs Forth was going to check for me.

Barbara Dorothy may have picked it up and put it somewhere.

Richard And what about this, then? (*He brandishes the book*) With his girlfriend's writing in it?

Mary That's what we were trying to tell you. It isn't her writing.

Richard (*taken aback*) It isn't? (*He looks at Eric*)

Eric (*helplessly*) I wouldn't know. I mean, we weren't in the habit of writing to each other. We were meeting almost every day so there was never the need. I wouldn't recognize her writing if I saw it.

Barbara We think it belonged to one of your locums. Dr Ellis. He must have left it behind.

Richard Ellis? (*He tries to recall him*) The fellow from Bedford with sweaty socks and halitosis? (*He looks at the book*) This is his?

Barbara nods

(*Uncomfortably*) So all that fuss was ... (*To Eric; embarrassed*) Looks like I owe you an apology.

Eric (*stiffly*) It wouldn't come amiss. I came here yesterday in all good faith, but as soon as I realized my mistake, I apologized and left. What this is about, I don't know, but if you wouldn't mind finding out about my pen, I'll be out of your hair for good.

Richard It wasn't a Sheaffer, was it? I found one in the hall when I came in last night. Popped it in the desk.

Richard moves to the desk, puts the book down and finds the pen

This the one? (*He hands it to Eric*)

Eric (*examining it briefly and nodding*) Thank you.

Richard (*awkwardly*) Look. I'm sorry about all this. No hard feelings, eh?

Eric (*tightly*) Of course not. (*He puts the pen in his pocket*)

Barbara (*relieved*) You will stay for a cup of tea? (*She turns back to the tray*)

Eric (*shaking his head*) No, thanks. I'd better be off. I need to reach London by eleven.

Barbara (*surprised*) I thought you were in Ilfracombe 'til Sunday?

Eric I should have been. But I finished the last deal in this area over breakfast so there's no need to hang around. London's my next port of call.

Richard (*abashed*) I'll see you out then. And I'm sorry about the misunderstanding.

Eric (*stiffly*) Yes. (*To Mary and Allan*) Been nice meeting you. Bye. (*He moves to the door*)

Barbara (*to Richard; impulsively*) I'll do it. You see to the teas.

Eric exits and Barbara follows him out of the room

Richard (*embarrassed*) Sorry about all that. Not often I lose my temper.

Allan (*sagely*) Happens to the best of us.

Mary (*smiling*) And there's no harm done, is there?

Richard begins pouring tea

Richard It's just been so damned frustrating trying to convince her I'd never heard of this Grace Walker woman. And all she could do was wave that blasted book at me as if it were the Holy Grail.

Mary (*soothingly*) Well, it's all over now and it's been sorted. But it does show how things can get when they're blown out of proportion.

Allan We had something similar at the Bowling Club a few years back.

Mary (*in disbelief*) Allan. Will you please shut up about the Bowling Club?

Richard brings tea down for them

Richard (*amused*) I did say he could tell me about the Guineaford match.

Mary (*taking her cup*) Well, I don't want to hear about it again. I've heard it twice already. And so has Barbara.

Barbara enters

Barbara So has Barbara, what?

Mary (*glancing round*) I'm just saying if they're going to start talking bowls, we're going into the kitchen.

Barbara Good idea. I'll just pour myself a cup and we can take it through. (*Pouring herself a cup and adding milk from the second jug; to Richard*) By the way. You didn't take my car, did you? I'm a bit low on fuel.

Richard What else could I do? Mine's still at the garage. (*To Allan*) Took it in Thursday and I'm still waiting for the estimate. (*To Barbara*) But you're all right. I filled up last night.

Barbara (*looking up*) Sorry?

Richard On the way to Combe Martin. I could hardly walk there, could I?

Barbara (*smiling*) No. Of course not. I wasn't thinking. Anyone like a biscuit?

The door chimes sound

Richard (*groaning*) Not another call out.

Barbara I'll get it.

Barbara puts her cup down and exits

Richard If it's that blasted Dixon woman again …

Mary (*knowingly*) Not on a Saturday night, Richard.

Allan She'll be bingoing at South Molton with their Sarah. Hasn't missed a game in five years according to what she says.

Mary (*amused*) I wouldn't mind so much, but she's always complaining they can't afford things. And they both drink and smoke like troopers.

Barbara enters followed by Dorothy, who wears an outdoor coat and carries a collection of shopping bags

Barbara Only Dorothy.

Dorothy (*laughing*) Not so much of the "only". I'm not stopping, but I was just on my way back from Barnstaple so I thought I'd drop in and see how things were. (*To Allan and Mary*) She wasn't too well after you went yesterday.

Barbara (*hastily*) But I'm fine, now. Fine. And everything's worked itself out. Will you have a cup of tea?

Dorothy (*gratefully*) I wouldn't say no. I was waiting ages for the bus, and there was another accident on the Link Road according to the driver. (*She puts her bags down*)

Barbara (*picking up the teapot*) Oh. (*She peers inside it*) I'll boil some more water.

Dorothy No. Don't bother, then. I'll be home in a few minutes.

Barbara puts down the teapot and picks up her own cup

Barbara Have this one. I've not touched it, yet.
Richard (*sharply*) But that's soya milk, isn't it?
Dorothy (*taking the cup and saucer*) Doesn't bother me. It's what we were drinking yesterday.
Mary Soya milk?
Barbara Oh, yes. I'm not allowed the real stuff. (*With mock severity*) No dairy products for Mrs Forth. Doctor's orders. (*Ruefully*) That's why I didn't have the cream cake this afternoon.
Allan (*remembering*) And you had black coffee.
Mary (*doubtfully*) I don't think I'd fancy soya milk. What does it taste like?
Barbara Not much different from ordinary. (*To Dorothy*) Don't you think?
Dorothy I don't mind it, really. (*She sips at the tea then pulls a face*) But I think this is off. (*She holds the cup towards Barbara*)
Barbara (*puzzled*) Off? (*She looks into the cup, then sniffs at it*) It shouldn't be. I only opened it this morning.
Dorothy (*wiping her lips*) Doesn't taste right, though. It's sort of, I don't know — *peculiar.*
Barbara (*frowning*) I am sorry. I'll get some fresh.
Richard (*genially*) It's all right. I'll do it. Have to make a call, anyway.

Richard takes the cup from Dorothy, picks up the teapot and jug and exits

Dorothy (*slightly embarrassed*) Sorry about that, but I could tell there was something wrong the minute I tasted it. I've always had sensitive taste buds. Most people probably wouldn't have noticed.
Mary I know I wouldn't. I was telling Barbara this afternoon. I can hardly taste anything since I had the flu. Takes all the fun out of a black forest gateau.
Allan Doesn't stop you eating them, though, does it? (*To Dorothy*) You should have seen the slice this afternoon. They could have fed those starving Africans for a month on it.
Mary (*protesting*) Allan. That's not very nice.

Dorothy suddenly sways and puts a hand to her head

(*Noticing*) Dorothy?

Barbara (*startled*) Are you all right? (*She moves to her*)

Mary (*putting her cup and saucer down*) You're white as a sheet.

Barbara (*supporting Dorothy*) Here. Sit down. (*She leads her to the easy chair*)

Allan (*rising*) Do you want me to get Richard?

Barbara (*to Dorothy; anxiously*) Are you feeling sick? Have you eaten anything unusual?

Dorothy (*with an effort*) Slice of cream cake. But that was this afternoon.

Barbara We'd better have Richard take a look at you. Just to be on the safe side.

Dorothy attempts to rise but Barbara holds her down

No. Stay where you are. He'll be here in a second. (*To Allan*) Try and find Colin and tell him what's happened.

Barbara hurries to the door and exits

(*Off*) Richard? Richard?

Mary hurries to Dorothy's side and crouches beside her

Mary It's all right, Dorothy. You're in good hands.

Allan (*hovering helplessly*) You'll be right as rain in no time.

Dorothy closes her eyes and slumps

Mary (*anxiously*) Dorothy? (*More insistently*) Dorothy? (*She turns her head; calling out*) Richard? Richard?

Barbara hurries in

Barbara He's on his way. (*She rushes over to them*) What is it? What's wrong?

Mary (*in disbelief*) I think she's *gone*.

They all look at Dorothy in horror

Richard hurries back into the room. He crosses to the women as the Lights fade

CURTAIN

ACT II
Scene 1

The same. The following Wednesday. Early afternoon

The curtains are open, the room is neat and tidy and the electric fire is on low

Richard sits at the desk writing and light, classical music plays softly

After a few moments the doorbell chimes are heard. Richard hesitates, then puts down his pen, stands and exits

Richard (*after a moment; off*) Julia. Come in.

There is a slight pause then Richard enters, followed by Julia. She wears an expensive looking summer coat, carries a handbag over her arm and clutches a glossy cardboard cake box, tied with a pink ribbon

Julia (*glancing around*) All alone?

Richard (*crossing to the music centre and turning it off*) She's at the hospital visiting Dorothy. Sit yourself down.

Julia (*moving in front of the settee*) And how is she? The invalid, I mean.

Richard (*moving to the drinks table*) As well as can be expected. But she'll be out of circulation for a while. Can I get you a drink?

Julia A sherry would be nice. It's colder out there than it looks.

As he pours the drinks, Julia puts the cake box and her handbag on the settee and moves to the fireplace, unfastening her coat

They tell me you saved her life.

Richard You shouldn't believe everything you hear.

Julia But according to Mary Haigh ——

Richard (*drily*) It's a good job this village doesn't rely on Mary Haigh for medical attention. It was a minor stroke, she lost consciousness, but she's going to be fine. (*Moving down to her with the drinks*) Now let's change the subject, shall we, because I can't discuss my patients with anyone outside the profession, as you very well know. (*He hands her the sherry*)

Julia (*smiling*) Quite right, too. I'd hate to have my problem circulating this place. I can see the pursed lips already. That's why I'm having it done in Switzerland.

Richard You needn't have bothered, you know. I could have put you in touch with a number of British clinics. Discretion assured.

Julia I know you could, darling, but this is the way I want it. False identity, secret clinic … and a few weeks recuperation in some luxurious hotel before my triumphant return to the social scene.

Richard (*amused*) And am I to know how to contact you if anything crops up?

Julia (*archly*) No. There's not a soul in the world who'll know where I am. I'll just fly in as usual, then vanish into thin air until I'm ready to face the world again. (*She smiles*) But don't worry. I'll contact you as soon as it's over. I promise. (*Remembering*) Oh. And by the way. (*She moves to the settee and picks up the cake box*) These are for you. (*She turns and holds it out to him*)

Richard puts his glass on the mantelpiece and takes the cake box

Richard Maison Bervoix?

Julia A little "thank you" for signing my passport photos.

Richard (*embarrassed*) There was no need.

Julia I know. But I was passing the shop and remembered how much you liked them. (*She sits on the settee and sips at her sherry*)

Richard (*smiling*) If there's one advantage to living in Bere Knighton, it's the close proximity of Maison Bervoix. What that couple can do to a handful of fruit and flour's an absolute miracle. Thank you.

Julia I've even included a special one for Barbara so she wouldn't feel left out. You did say she was off dairy produce?

Richard (*nodding*) For the moment. Yes. I'll put them in the kitchen.

Richard begins to move off

Julia (*suddenly*) There is something else, Richard.

Richard (*halting*) Oh?

Julia What you were saying on Saturday. About Barbara.

Richard (*moving down to her; puzzled*) Yes?

Julia You were serious, weren't you? If she wasn't here, you'd marry me.

Richard (*uncomfortably*) Look, Julia, I wasn't exactly thinking straight. We'd had a bad time …

Julia (*pressing*) But you did say you would, didn't you? You did say that?

Richard Well, yes. But I've already explained ——

Julia (*soothingly*) It's all right. I'm not making an issue of it. I just wanted to be sure.

Richard Sure?

Julia That I've done the right thing.

Julia puts her glass on the settee arm, opens her handbag and takes out a long, slim envelope

This is for you. I'd like you to hold it for me. (*She holds it out to him*)

Richard (*taking it*) What is it?

Julia My new will. If anything happens to me — a plane crash or anything — I've left everything to you. The house. The money. Everything. (*She picks up her glass again and sips*)

Richard (*puzzled*) But, why?

Julia When Malcolm died eight years ago, he left me quite a substantial amount. I believe I invested it wisely. According to my accountant, I'm now worth somewhere in the region of three million pounds.

Richard (*stunned*) I'd no idea.

Julia (*amused*) I'm sure you hadn't. I've never broadcast my financial situation to the local gossipmongers and have no intention of starting now. This is for your ears alone. But let me finish. (*She sips her sherry*) After giving it some thought, I decided to put my affairs in order and make you my sole beneficiary.

Richard (*in shock*) But …

Julia (*offhandedly*) I've no family. No relations. No favourite causes. And I've certainly no intention of letting the government sink its grubby little claws into it, so who else would I leave it to? (*Pointedly*) But as our American cousins like to say — there's no such thing as a free lunch. There is a condition.

Richard Which is?

Julia (*rising*) I want *you*, Richard. I've wanted you for years. And if it hadn't been for your ridiculous infatuation with Barbara, well — that's water under the bridge, isn't it? But I want your solemn promise that if anything happens to her, you'll marry me at the earliest opportunity. (*She pauses*) Is that such a terrible thing to ask?

Richard (*stunned*) No. No. Of course not. But I ——

Julia (*briskly*) Then it's all settled. (*She glances at her watch*) Quarter past four. I'd better be going. (*She finishes her drink, hands him the glass and begins to fasten her coat*) I'll be in Norwich for the next few weeks and I'm leaving tonight. I'll be heading for Berne from there, so I won't see you again 'til everything's over. (*Casually*) I, er, don't suppose you could call round before I go? Just for a farewell drink?

Richard (*apologetically*) It's the charity social thing. Down at the hall.

Julia (*coldly*) Oh, yes. I'd forgotten. And of course, you have to be there.

Richard (*grimacing*) I'm doing the vote of thanks.

Julia I see. (*She smiles tightly*) No matter. Perhaps another time. (*She picks up her handbag*)

Richard (*suddenly*) I could make an excuse.

Julia (*still cold*) There's really no need.

Richard But I want to. I was going to be late anyway.

Julia (*quietly triumphant*) Well, in that case we'll say seven o'clock, shall we?

Richard Seven it is.

Julia (*smiling*) I'll be waiting for you. (*She kisses him lightly and moves to the door*) Give my love to Barbara. And enjoy the cakes.

Julia exits

For a moment Richard stands there looking at the door, then looks at the envelope in his hand. Putting the cake box on the settee, he hesitates, then opens the envelope takes out the will and reads it. After doing so, he slowly lowers it, looking stunned

Richard (*softly*) Millions.

The sound of the telephone in the hall snaps him back to reality and he drops the will on to the settee and exits

(*Off*) Hello? … Yes. … Yes. I did them this morning. You can collect them tonight during surgery. … No, tomorrow's all right. I'll leave them at reception. Any time after eight thirty.

Barbara (*off*) Oooh, it's freezing out there. Whoever called this flaming June? Oh, sorry. Sorry.

Barbara enters the room. She is wearing a light outdoor coat. Crossing behind the settee to the fireplace, she turns up the electric fire and begins to unfasten her coat

Richard (*off*) No. There's no charge. It's all part of the service. … Sorry? … No. No. I don't think so. Malaria's not exactly a problem in Disneyworld.

Slipping off her coat, Barbara drapes it on the settee back then notices the will and the cake box

(*Off; after a pause*) Yes. Yes. I'm sure she did. But Africa's a long way from Florida.

Barbara frowns, picks up the will and glances at it

(*Off; after a pause*) Well, I'm quite sure the American health regulations are just as stringent as ours. … Yes. But your insurance should cover that. If you just check the details …

Barbara's face registers disbelief

Then I suggest you increase it. The whole thing's very unlikely anyway. … It's entirely up to you. … Yes. Yes. As you say — it's best not to take chances. Goodbye.

Barbara quickly replaces the will on the settee and turns to the fire, warming her hands

Richard hastily enters the room and relaxes when he sees her

Blasted Dixon woman again. Can't afford prescription charges, but a fortnight in Florida, well — that's a different proposition altogether. (*He snatches up the will and stuffs it in his pocket*) How's Dorothy?

Barbara (*turning to him*) She still looks dreadful. But she can't wait to get home again. The woman in the next bed's driving her mad. (*She notices the will has gone*)

Richard (*bluffly*) Well, she'll be out by the weekend, all being well. (*Awkwardly*) Oh, and about tonight. Something's come up.

Barbara (*dismayed*) Don't say you're not going to make it?

Richard (*turning away*) Of course not. I'll just be a little late, that's all.

Barbara (*plaintively*) How late?

Richard (*irritated*) I've no idea. I'll be there as soon as I can. All right? (*He returns to the desk, sits and picks up his pen*)

Barbara Is it anything I can help with?

Richard If it was, I'd have asked you. Look. I've already said I'll be there.

Barbara (*picking up her coat*) Well, I hope you are, Richard Forth. Because I'm not doing your speech if they call your name and you're missing.

Richard (*writing*) It's not a speech, it's a vote of thanks. And there's no danger of me being missing. Old Caswell can talk the hind leg off a donkey. He'll still be babbling when the rest of us have turned into pumpkins.

Barbara (*lightly*) That's not nice, Richard. I like Bernard Caswell. We should have him on local radio.

Richard Yes. And then we could turn him off.

Barbara (*picking up the cake box*) And what's this? (*She displays it*)

Richard (*looking up*) Exactly what it says on top. Cakes from Maison Bervoix. Courtesy of Julia Moore. And before you say anything, there's a dairy-free item for you.

Barbara (*fishing*) So, to what do we owe the honour?

Richard (*writing again*) Signing her passport photos.

Barbara (*looking at him askance*) Is that all?

Richard What else could there be?

Barbara (*shrugging*) How should I know? (*Lightly*) You might be having a mad, passionate affair with her.

Richard (*irritated*) Don't be ridiculous.

Barbara (*relenting*) Well, I may not like the woman, but I certainly admire her taste. We'll have them now, shall we? With a nice cup of tea. I'll put the kettle on.

Barbara exits, carrying the cake box

Richard continues writing for a moment, then he puts down his pen and takes a medical book from the top of the desk and opens it. He searches the pages intently, checks an entry, then closes the book and replaces it with a thoughtful expression on his face

Barbara enters

Barbara By the way. I saw Mrs Eastment in Bradley's. Apparently Tony's perking up a little and complaining about having to stay in bed. Is there any chance of him being up and about before the 26th?

Richard (*absently*) I'll drop in and see her later.

Barbara (*frowning*) Is something wrong?

Richard (*shaking his head*) No. No. Just an idea …

Barbara (*lightly*) Must be a painful one. You look like you've swallowed a wasp.

The door chimes sound

I'll get it.

Barbara exits

(*Off*) Allan.

Allan   (*off*) Sorry to bother you, Barbara, but we've got a bit of a problem.

Barbara   (*off*) Come in.

Allan   (*off*) No. I won't stop. I just wanted a quick word. It's about tonight.

Barbara   (*off*) Well, I'm sure you can tell me inside. It's like winter out there.

Allan   (*off*) I've not had time to notice, really. I've been dashing around like a headless chicken since half eleven this morning. No, what I'm calling for is, I was wondering if you'd help in the kitchen tonight if Mary can't make it?

Allan enters, followed by Barbara

I've just been to ask Phyllis Longstaff, but she's visiting her daughter in Colchester, and Molly Wilks and Ruth Chatto don't get on — so we're a bit stuck.

Barbara   Of course I will. But what's wrong? Has something happened?

Allan   She had a bit of a tumble this morning. Tripped on the pavement outside Mostyns and took the skin off her knees. Right mess, it looks.

Barbara   (*wincing*) Oh, no.

Richard   (*rising*) Would you like me to take a look at her?

Allan   (*shaking his head*) She's more embarrassed than anything. We've cleaned all the grazes with antiseptic and put bandages on.

Richard   All the same. It wouldn't do any harm. I'll get my case.

Richard exits

Allan   (*to Barbara*) Tell you the truth. She's more upset about maybe missing tonight.

Barbara   (*reassuringly*) Well, perhaps it won't come to that. There's still a few hours. (*She sighs*) But isn't it always the way? One step forward and two steps back. How on earth did she manage it? Falling over, I mean? It wasn't a cracked paving stone?

Allan   No. No. Nothing like that. She just wasn't looking. Well, to tell you the truth, she thought she saw somebody. You know? Somebody she wasn't expecting. She only turned her head for a second and over she went.

Barbara (*curiously*) Who was it?

Allan The young fellow who called here, last week.

Barbara (*startled*) Mr Dawson? (*Frowning*) But it couldn't have been. He went to London.

Allan (*nodding*) That's what I said. But she's convinced it was him crossing the junction.

Barbara (*frowning*) Then maybe it was. I mean — he could have come back — though I don't know why. I shouldn't think there's anything in Bere Knighton to attract him.

Allan Well, I didn't see him myself and we all know her eyes aren't what they used to be. She can hardly see from one end of the green to the other, these days. (*He shakes his head*) Mistaken identity, if you ask me. She'll perhaps keep her mind on where she's going, next time.

Barbara (*kindly*) I expect she's pretty shaken, though. (*Brightening*) But I know what'll put a smile on her face. Julia Moore dropped in this afternoon with cakes from Maison Bervoix. I'm sure Mary can make better use of them than we can.

Allan (*protesting*) Oh, no. No.

Barbara (*smiling*) It'll be a consolation prize if the worst comes to the worst. We've still half a lemon cake to satisfy our cravings. And if I can't eat cream, I'm damned if I'm going to let Richard do it.

Richard enters, carrying his medical case

I'll just get them for you.

Richard Get what?

Barbara The cakes Julia left us. I'm giving them to Allan and Mary. You don't mind, do you?

Richard (*irritated*) Of course I mind. They're supposed to be for us.

Barbara (*lightly*) I know. I know. But it won't kill us to do without, will it? Think of all those nasty little calories we'll be avoiding. (*Chiding*) And don't give me that hard-done-by look, Richard. If there's one of Mrs Jackson's trifles on offer tonight, you'll eat twice as much of it as anyone else, and don't tell me you won't.

Barbara exits

Allan (*embarrassed*) I'm sorry about this, Richard

Richard (*shaking his head*) She's always giving things away. It's like being married to Lady Bountiful. If we've got it, she can always find someone to give it to. Thank God she's no idea what …

Richard suddenly halts

Allan What?

Richard (*shaking his head*) Doesn't matter. It's nothing important. (*Changing the subject*) So how's Jennifer, these days? Still robbing graves in Egypt?

Allan (*relaxing*) Last thing we heard. They've found bits of bone and all sorts in the place they're at now. Way she goes on about it, you'd think they were digging out diamonds. Don't see the attraction myself, but she's happy as a sandboy. (*Frowning*) Though there is a rumour they might have to move out if plans go ahead for the new dam.

Richard I'd have thought they'd learned their lesson with the last one they built out there. It's caused more problems than the droughts it was meant to prevent.

Allan Well, there's nothing concrete — if you'll excuse the pun. And it'll be good to see her again if she does come home. It's been a few years now, and there's neither of us getting any younger.

Barbara enters with the cake box

Barbara (*brightly*) Who are we talking about?

Richard Allan's daughter.

Barbara (*interested*) She's not coming home, is she?

Allan (*hastily*) No, no. Not that we know of, anyway.

Barbara (*handing Allan the cake box*) Good job. There's only the two of them in here. Well, one and three quarters, actually. (*Embarrassed*) I couldn't resist a teensy-weensy slice from the end of mine.

Richard (*disgustedly*) Talk about giving away your cake and eating it.

Barbara (*grimacing*) Sorry.

Richard (*to Allan*) We'd better make a run for it before she changes her mind and gobbles the rest.

The telephone rings in the hall

Barbara (*hastily*) I'll get it.

Barbara hurriedly exits, leaving the door ajar

Richard (*calling*) If it's for me, I've just gone out.

Barbara (*off*) Hello? … Well, yes. But he's … Oh, dear. Hold on a second.

Barbara appears in the doorway holding the telephone

The Cow and Calf in East Molton. One of their guests has collapsed. They think it's a heart attack. Wife tells them there's a history.

Richard (*scowling*) More likely food poisoning if the last meal I had at that place is anything to go by. (*Resignedly*) All right. Tell them not to move him. I'll be there in ten minutes.

Barbara exits

(*To Allan*) Sorry about this. I'll call in on Mary later.
Allan You don't have to. It's nothing to worry about.
Richard Let me decide that. (*He glances at the cake box*) Enjoy the cakes.

Richard exits

The outside door slams

A moment later Barbara enters

Barbara That's the second one this week (*Hastily*) Not at *The Cow and Calf*. I mean the second tourist. I think they come to Devon especially to have heart attacks.
Allan (*sagely*) Wouldn't surprise me. There was a couple in Dendy's this morning bought every tub of clotted cream they could lay their hands on. Good job we'd ordered our lot for tonight, or they'd have had that as well.
Barbara (*grinning*) And that would have upset Richard. Especially after losing out on those. (*She nods at the cake box*) That fruit cake's out of this world.
Allan (*uncomfortable*) I don't have to take them, you know.
Barbara (*firmly*) You certainly do. They'll cheer Mary up no end.

The door chimes sound

(*Rolling her eyes*) Now who's that?

Barbara exits into the hall

(*Off; surprised*) Mr Dawson.
Eric (*off; urgently*) I know I'm the last person you expected, but I've got to have a word with you. It's very important. May I come in?
Barbara (*off; hesitantly*) Well — yes.

Eric enters

Eric If I'm making a fool of myself, you'll have to forgive me but …

(*He notices Allan*) Oh.

Barbara enters behind Eric

(*To Barbara*) I'm sorry. I didn't realize you had company.
Barbara (*frowning*) What is it? Is something wrong?
Eric (*glancing at Allan uncomfortably*) It's a bit … delicate.
Allan (*hastily*) I'm just on my way.

Allan begins to move

Barbara (*to Allan*) No. Wait.

Allan halts and looks uncomfortable

(*To Eric*) Is it Richard you're looking for?
Eric (*shaking his head*) I'm afraid your husband's the last person I want
     to see, Mrs Forth. And to be quite honest, I … Look, I — I'll call back
     some other time, shall I? It might be *better*.
Barbara (*puzzled*) I don't understand. I thought you'd gone to
     London.
Eric I had. But something turned up that made me come back again. I'll
     explain later. Perhaps tonight?
Barbara I won't be here tonight. I'm helping at a social in the village
     hall. What's wrong with now?
Eric (*glancing at Allan again*) It's not something I can say in front of
     witnesses.

Both Allan and Barbara react

(*Earnestly*) If I'm wrong, I could find myself in trouble. But I've got
     to know the truth … and you're the only one who can help me.
Barbara (*puzzled*) I'm sorry?
Eric (*attempting to exit*) I'll speak to you later.
Barbara (*firmly*) No, Mr Dawson. Whatever it is you have to say, I
     want to hear it now.
Eric (*protesting*) But I've already told you …
Barbara You haven't told me anything. In fact, the only thing I do
     know is that whatever bee's buzzing in your bonnet, you don't want
     my husband to know about it. So hadn't you better explain before he
     gets back?
Allan (*embarrassed*) I think I'll be off. Mary'll wonder where I've got
     to.

Barbara I'd rather you didn't, Allan. Unlike Mr Dawson here, I think I'd be glad of a witness. (*To Eric*) Well?

Eric (*awkwardly*) I don't know quite how to say this ...

Barbara I understand English rather well.

Eric (*flushing*) I mean it's not easy. We hardly know each other and there's no reason in the world for you to believe a word I say. But the top and bottom of it is ... (*Floundering*) Well ... (*Blurting it out*) I think you're in danger!

Barbara and Allan exchange surprised looks

(*Hastily*) I can't prove it. There's no actual evidence. But I have to warn you. Before it's too late.

Barbara (*after a pause*) What do you mean? Danger?

Eric (*hesitantly*) Someone may be planning to kill you.

Barbara and Allan react

Barbara Kill me?

Allan (*to Barbara*) He's out of his mind. Who'd want to kill you?

Eric (*urgently*) As I said. I can't prove anything. But I know there's something wrong. I know he's been lying.

Barbara (*baffled*) Who has?

Eric (*blurting it out*) Your husband. (*Quietly*) I think he's a murderer.

Barbara looks at him in disbelief

Allan (*grimly*) Now that's enough. I don't know what your game is, young fellow, but the sooner you drop it and get out of here, the better.

Eric (*quickly*) Just give me a minute. Let me say what I have to and I'll be gone like a shot.

Allan (*angrily*) We don't want to hear it. And if you're not on your way in the next few seconds, I'll throw you out myself. (*He puts the cake box down*)

Eric (*desperately; to Barbara*) Thirty seconds. It could save your life.

Allan (*advancing on Eric*) Right.

Barbara (*recovering herself*) No, Allan. Let me handle this.

Allan glares at Eric

(*To Eric; coldly*) All right, Mr Dawson. You've got one minute to prove you're not suffering from some sort of delusion concerning my husband, and convince me my life's in danger. After that, I'll be phoning the police and telling them the full story. Is that clear?

Eric (*nodding*) Absolutely. Do you mind if I sit down?

Barbara does not reply so he sits on the settee

I suppose it all started last week. Thinking I'd tracked Grace down here, then finding out I'd made a complete fool of myself. I was still smarting when I got back to Ilfracombe and even blamed myself for stepping in front of the car that nearly killed me later that night. At least, until I came here the second time — to look for my pen.

Barbara (*glancing at her wristwatch*) Forty-five seconds.

Eric (*hurrying on*) It was when you showed me out, you see? I saw it again. Right outside the house. A black Volvo with some kind of poster in the rear window.

Barbara (*unflinchingly*) I'm sorry to shatter your illusion, Mr Dawson, but that happens to be my car. And it hasn't been to Ilfracombe in months.

Eric I'm sorry, but I think you're wrong. There's no way I could mistake it.

Allan And why's that? The last time you came here, you told us you only caught a glimpse of it.

Eric I did. But I also noticed the near-side rear light had been taped up — like the one outside — and combined with that poster ...

Barbara (*scornfully*) There must be dozens of Volvo's in this part of the world with damaged rear lights, Mr Dawson. And most of them will be sporting posters of one kind or another.

Eric (*tightly*) But most of them didn't try to run me over.

Barbara (*after a pause*) So where does my husband come into this?

Eric He was the one who drove it. He was trying to kill me.

Barbara (*amused*) And why should he want to do that?

Eric (*quietly*) Because I came here looking for Grace. (*Hurrying on*) Oh, I didn't realize it at once. I was still trying to convince myself I'd made a mistake. I was halfway to London before it dawned on me. But once I'd put it together, I knew.

Barbara Knew?

Eric He'd been lying. He did know Grace, and for some reason he didn't want anyone to know about it. That's when I started getting curious. You can find almost anything out if you know the right place to look. So I started digging and came up with some interesting information. Did you know, for instance, he'd been married before?

Barbara Of course I knew. His first wife's name was Nancy and she died in a boating accident several years ago.

Eric Did he tell you that?

Barbara (*firmly*) Yes.

Eric And did he also tell you the local police strongly suspected him of arranging the accident?

Barbara stares at him, dumbfounded

Apparently they'd taken out very large life insurances a few months earlier. The case was only dropped when enquiries failed to turn up any *real* evidence and the good doctor sold his practice to leave town. The last anyone saw of him, he was heading for Italy. It's all in the *Daily Mail*. I took photocopies.

Allan And what's that supposed to prove? Absolutely nothing. He's a good man is Richard Forth, and we all know what the papers are like. They're never happy unless they're blackening somebody's good name. Mostly those who least deserve it.

Eric Maybe you're right, Mr … Haines.

Allan (*tartly*) Haigh.

Eric (*softly*) But then there's Grace.

Barbara (*firmly*) Grace Walker ——

Eric Was my fiancée. I told you what had happened the first time I came here. But what I didn't know then, was that the only place I would find her was in Dover Cemetery. She was buried there eight years ago. While I was still in Canada.

Barbara (*frowning*) Then what … ?

Eric They found her a few miles up the coast. She'd been in the water for days and it took some time to find out who she was and what she was doing in Kent. (*Quietly*) An hotel manager finally identified her. Apparently she'd booked a room, expecting her fiancée to join her, and the last time anyone saw her alive, she was heading for the station to meet his train. But as no-one knew who he was, and he never showed up at the hotel, the coroner decided she'd killed herself when he failed to arrive and recorded a verdict of suicide. There were only a few pounds in her bank account and with no living relatives, the local authority were left to bury her. Which gave me another shock.

Barbara Oh?

Eric You see, when I got back to England, I found she'd sold her father's business before she left — for over a million pounds. So what happened to it? Where had it gone?

Barbara Didn't anyone make enquiries?

Eric I've no idea. It's not even mentioned in the papers. (*Bitterly*) But Grace is buried in a pauper's grave.

Allan (*bluntly*) And what's this to do with Richard?

Eric (*coldly*) I think I told you the first time I came here. One of her neighbours told me she'd gone off to Devon to marry a Doctor Forth, but after I came here and drew a blank, I checked with the BMA. They told me there was only one practitioner of that name in Devon and that was Richard Forth of Bere Knighton. (*To Barbara*) Your husband.

Barbara (*tightly*) So why didn't this helpful neighbour inform the police?

Eric She was never asked. And the only reason she remembered his name was because her mother's maiden name also happened to be Forth.

Barbara (*fuming*) And out of all this farrago, you've decided that a perfectly innocent man is some kind of — of — Bluebeard and I'm to be his next victim? (*Icily*) I think you'd better *leave*, Mr Dawson. And if you mention one word of this ridiculous accusation to anyone else, we'll sue for every penny you've got. Is that understood? (*She glares at him*)

Eric (*rising; defeated*) I knew you'd never believe me. You don't understand what some people will do to get their hands on someone else's money.

Barbara (*frostily*) The matter doesn't arise in my case. I doubt there's more than a few hundred pounds in my personal account. And even if there were, I'd willingly turn it over to him should he ask. So good-bye, Mr Dawson, and please don't bother me again.

Eric hesitates, then exits, followed by a grim Barbara

A moment later, the front door is heard to close firmly and Barbara enters looking unsteady

Allan (*disgustedly*) Well I've heard some stories. Don't you think we should call the police?

Barbara (*weakly*) No. No. Let it go. There's no harm done. He's obviously round the bend (*Suddenly clutching her stomach in pain*) Oohhhh.

Allan (*alarmed; moving to her*) What is it? What's wrong?

Barbara (*forcing a smile*) Just the old tummy playing up. It must be the upset.

Allan (*helping her to the settee*) Here. Sit yourself down. I'll make you a cup of tea.

Barbara (*protesting weakly*) No, no. You get back to Mary. I'll be fine now he's gone. Honestly. (*She groans again*)

Allan (*concerned*) You look terrible.

Barbara (*joking painfully*) Pale and interesting.

She suddenly retches, covers her mouth and stumbles in the direction of the door

Allan (*alarmed*) Barbara.

Barbara quickly exits

Allan stands there looking worried, then hurries to the desk and starts searching through the various papers cluttering it. As he does so, the front door slams shut and Richard's voice is heard

Richard (*off*) Bloody bogus phone calls. That's the second one in a week.

The door is flung open and Richard storms into the room

Hadn't a clue what I was talking about when I got there. They've not even got any guests. The whole place is being redécor —— (*He notices Allan*) What the hell are you doing?
Allan (*hastily*) I was looking to see if you had a mobile number. It's Barbara. She's not well.
Richard (*gritting his teeth*) Not again. And what's wrong with her this time? (*He deposits his case*)
Allan You'd better have a look at her. It happened just after that Dawson chap left.
Richard (*frowning*) Dawson? The computer man? From last week? What's he doing back?
Allan Well, it's not my place to say — but if I were you, I'd get the police in to deal with him, PDQ.
Richard (*sharply*) Police? What are you talking about?
Allan He made some quite nasty accusations. Said you'd murdered your first wife as well as this Grace woman he was looking for ... and Barbara might be next in line.

Richard gapes at Allan

I think that's what triggered her off.
Richard (*angrily*) I'll trigger him off. Where is he? Where did he go?
Allan He's just left. About a minute ago.
Richard (*grimly*) Right. I'll soon put a stop to this. (*He heads for the door*)
Allan (*calling*) What about Barbara?
Richard (*as he goes*) Make her a cup of tea.

Richard exits

Allan stands motionless as the outside door slams

The Lights fade to Black-out

SCENE 2

The same. Friday morning

The cake box and medical case have been removed and the fire has been switched off, but apart from that the room is untouched and empty. After a moment, there is the sound of door chimes. Nothing happens. The chimes sound again

Barbara (*off; wearily*) All right. All right. I'm coming. Give me a chance.

There is a slight pause

Dorothy (*off; brightly*) Surprise.
Barbara (*off*) Dorothy. I didn't know you were home. (*Hastily*) Come in. Come in. How are you? When did they let you out?
Dorothy (*off; concerned*) Never mind me. What about you? You look awful.

A wan looking Barbara enters wearing pyjamas, housecoat and slippers. She is followed by a slow moving Dorothy who wears a light coat over her dress

Barbara (*drily*) Thanks for the kind words. I'll recommend you.
Dorothy You know what I mean. (*Anxiously*) You're not ill again? I've not got you out of bed?
Barbara (*shaking her head*) I was just starting the shower, so stop looking guilty and sit yourself down. And yes. I have been sick but not like the last time. It was just a bug, according to Richard. Half the village's gone down with it.
Dorothy (*puzzled*) I'd not heard. (*She moves carefully to the settee, fumbling with her coat buttons*) Not that I've been out much since coming home. If Colin had his way, I'd spend the rest of my life in bed being waited on hand and foot. (*She opens her coat and sits*) He's like an old mother hen. Fuss, fuss, fuss. He nearly had my breakfast over his head this morning. (*Mockingly*) "Would you like me to cut your bacon for you, lover? Can you manage your egg all right?" (*In normal tones*) The minute he'd gone to work I got myself dressed and came out for a breath of fresh air.
Barbara (*kindly*) He has been worried.
Dorothy (*firmly*) Well he needn't have bothered himself. My aunt Bernice had two strokes — and lost the use of an arm — but she

looked after herself 'til the day she died. Besides, they wouldn't have sent me home if they'd thought I couldn't cope. It was only a minor one. What's bothering me is they want to put me on Warfarin, and I'm not sure I fancy swallowing stuff they use to keep the rat population down. (*Grinning*) Still, I can always slip it in his tea if he doesn't stop treating me like a piece of bone china.

Barbara (*smiling*) I'll put the kettle on, shall I? (*She turns to the door*)

Dorothy Not for me. My back teeth are floating, as Grandma Eccles used to say. He's been bringing me cups of tea since six this morning. (*Hastily*) But don't let me stop you.

Barbara No, no. I can have one later. When Richard gets back.

Dorothy (*curiously*) So when did it start, then, this epidemic?

Barbara (*remembering*) Oh, the stomach bug. (*Shrugging*) Wednesday night, I think. It did with me.

Dorothy (*aghast*) It wasn't the charity do, was it? You know. Food poisoning?

Barbara Oh, no. No. I never made it to that. Neither did Richard. Some of the cases were quite bad and he didn't get home 'til after eleven.

Dorothy Well I hope *she* got a nasty dose of it. It'll do her the world of good to have something in common with lesser mortals.

Barbara (*puzzled*) Sorry?

Dorothy Julia Moore. I'd been wondering what she called him out for. I saw him arrive.

Barbara (*frowning*) At Elm Cottage? Are you sure?

Dorothy (*nodding*) Oh, yes. It was just before seven. I'd been watching the news and Colin insisted I went to bed early with it being my first night home. You can see her place clear as day from the front bedroom. I sometimes feel like throwing rocks through her precious stained-glass windows.

Barbara (*frowning*) He never mentioned it.

Dorothy He wouldn't know, would he? I don't tell everybody … (*Realizing*) Oh, you mean about her being poorly? (*Shrugging*) Well, why should he, if everybody else is going down with it? Is that what's wrong with Allan?

Barbara gives her a puzzled look

Allan Haigh. They took him off in the ambulance about quarter to ten last night. Hadn't you heard?

Barbara I'd no idea. You're today's first caller.

Dorothy Mary was in a right state, according to Alice Timmins. He'd been sick on the living-room carpet, all down the hall and passed out cold in the bathroom.

Barbara (*shocked*) Oh, no.

Dorothy I thought I'd call later. To see how he was.

Barbara (*impulsively*) Give me a minute to shower and dress and I'll come with you.

Dorothy (*doubtfully*) Are you sure you feel up to it? You don't look too steady yourself.

Barbara Listen to who's talking. And anyway, I'm over the worst. If we go together at least we can support each other. (*She hesitates at the door*) Are you sure you don't want anything?

Dorothy I'm fine. Honestly.

Barbara Well, you know where everything is.

Barbara exits

Dorothy leans back on the settee and closes her eyes, obviously more weak than she admits. For a moment or two there is silence, then she sits up with a frown and fumbles in her coat pocket. Producing a small jar of honey, she looks at it and sighs

A moment later the door chimes sound and Dorothy carefully rises, replaces the honey jar in her pocket, crosses to the door and exits

Dorothy (*off*) I'll get it.

There is a short pause

Mary (*off; surprised*) Dorothy. I didn't know you were home.

Dorothy (*off*) Came out Wednesday. I think they were glad to get rid of me. (*Hastily*) Come in. Come in. Barbara'll be down in a minute. We were just on our way to see you. (*Concerned*) How's Allan?

Mary (*off; tired*) As well as can be expected, whatever that means.

Dorothy enters, followed by an exhausted looking Mary, whose knees are bandaged and who clutches a small suitcase

I suppose Richard told you?

Dorothy (*moving behind the settee*) It was Alice Timmins, actually. She mentioned it to Colin. I hadn't seen anybody 'til this morning. What happened?

Mary (*shaking her head*) I can't really say. One minute he was fine, and the next … He's going to be all right, though. They're sure of that. But until they get the results back …

Dorothy (*sympathetically*) You must be worried sick. I can't remember the last time either of you two were under the weather. (*She moves round to the front and sits*) Sit yourself down.

Mary I mustn't stay long. I only came home to pick up a few things and have a quick word with Barbara. (*She sits beside Dorothy and puts the case down*) Oh, Dorothy. He looks awful. All those tubes sticking out of him and his face white as a sheet.

Dorothy (*kindly*) It's probably not as bad as it seems. The woman in the bed opposite me looked like something out of a horror film when I came round, but three days later there she was, sitting in the day-room doing jigsaw puzzles. (*Patting Mary's hand*) I shouldn't upset yourself. They'll take good care of him.

Mary (*baffled*) But they seem to think it's food poisoning and I can't understand it. I mean — we had exactly the same to eat. If anything had been wrong, we'd both have been ill, wouldn't we?

Dorothy (*reassuringly*) Of course you would. But if they don't know yet, they're only guessing. It could be nothing to do with anything he's eaten. By the sound of it, it's more likely to be this bug that's doing the rounds. Half the village is down with it from what I've heard.

Mary (*blankly*) Is it?

Dorothy Oh, yes. Even Madame Moore hasn't escaped. She had to call Richard out, Wednesday night, so you know who to blame for him not turning up at the charity bash, don't you? He'd not have found her suffering in silence. There'd have been more drama in that place than the parson preached about.

Mary (*reproachfully*) That's not a very Christian remark, Dorothy.

Dorothy (*unabashed*) I don't *feel* particularly Christian where she's concerned. She causes more trouble 'round here with her airs and graces than foot and mouth ever did. If you ask me, it's a pity she came back.

Mary (*wryly*) She does seem to upset people, but I'm sure she doesn't mean to. It's just her way.

Dorothy (*scornfully*) Don't you fool yourself. She knows exactly what's she's doing, that one. (*Changing the subject*) But never mind her. (*She indicates Mary's knees*) What have you been up to?

Mary (*dismissive and embarrassed*) Oh, it's my own silly fault. I was so surprised at seeing that Dawson man, Wednesday morning, I didn't look where I was going.

Dorothy (*frowning*) You mean, the one who came here? To find his ex-girlfriend?

Mary Well — that was his story. But the way it turned out, he was a real wolf in sheep's clothing. It's a good job Barbara's tougher than she looks. She had him out of the house again before he could say knife.

Dorothy (*interested*) Have I been missing something?

Mary (*indignantly*) He only accused Richard of being a mass murderer. And told her she could be next on his list. If Allan hadn't heard it himself, I'd never have believed it.

Dorothy gapes at her

(*She glances anxiously at the door*) She won't be long, will she? I mustn't miss that bus.

Dorothy (*in disbelief*) But who did he think had been murdered?

Mary Richard's first wife, of course. Then this Walker woman he'd been going on about — and heaven knows how many others.

Dorothy (*puzzled*) But why?

Mary For their money, of course. (*Scornfully*) Have you ever heard the like?

Dorothy (*thoughtfully*) Well, there was Dr Crippen, wasn't there? And Dr Shipman.

Mary (*surprised*) You're not suggesting Richard's anything like those two?

Dorothy (*hastily*) No, no. Of course not. But it does make you think, doesn't it? She has been ill a lot. And nobody knew what was wrong with her. If you had a suspicious mind, you could easily jump to conclusions.

Mary (*firmly*) You'd need a sick mind to believe Richard Forth had anything to do with it. He worships the ground she walks on. (*Satisfied*) Still, he'll not be bothering them again, will he? Even though it wasn't a nice way to go.

Dorothy (*blankly*) I'm sorry?

Mary Off the road. He must have been doing eighty, at least, according to the police. Over an hour it took to get his body out.

Dorothy (*baffled*) Whose body?

Mary (*impatiently*) Eric Dawson's, of course. Whose did you think? (*She grimaces*) I'm glad it wasn't my job. They deserve medals, the ones who deal with that sort of thing.

Dorothy (*shocked*) I hadn't heard. I'd no idea. When did it happen?

Mary Wednesday night, they think. And they wouldn't have found him for days if the farmer hadn't been out with his dog. You'd think they'd do something about that road, wouldn't you? There's not a week goes by without somebody having an accident. And most of the time it's their own stupid fault. (*She sighs*) It's the families I feel sorry for.

Barbara enters, now dressed

Barbara (*concerned*) Oh, Mary. I'm so sorry about Allan.

Mary (*surprised*) It wasn't your fault, dear.

Barbara But he might have caught it from me. I was one of the first to go down with it.

Mary (*shaking her head*) They think it was food poisoning. But as I've just told Dorothy, we both had the same evening meal. Tuna and pasta bake with a salad. A glass of wine. And those little cakes you sent us.

Barbara (*frowning*) Cakes?

Mary From Maison Bervoir.

Barbara (*oddly*) You ate them last night?

Mary We didn't have time, *Wednesday*. What with the social and everything. And that's what I came to tell you. (*Pleased*) We raised six hundred and forty three pounds, all told, so there's no need to worry about not being there. Mr and Mrs Moody gave us a hand and Ruth Chatto swallowed her pride and dug in, so we coped quite well in the end. All I had to do was organize the coffee and I did that sitting down. (*Noticing Barbara's expression*) Is something wrong?

Barbara (*preoccupied*) No. No. I was thinking. (*Hesitantly*) Did — did they taste all right? The cakes, I mean.

Mary (*blankly*) They were lovely. Why?

Barbara Do you think it might have been the cream? That poisoned Allan.

Mary (*reassuringly*) Oh, no, dear. It wasn't that. And besides, I had the cream one. Allan had the fruit.

Barbara (*oddly*) The same as me.

Mary (*rising*) I'd best be off. But I'll call on the way back if you like and let you know how he is. (*She picks up the case then pauses*) If Richard has a spare minute, I'm sure he'd be glad to see him. Just for reassurance.

Barbara (*absently*) I'll tell him as soon as he gets here.

Mary (*easily*) I'll see myself out.

Mary exits

Barbara stands as if in a trance

Dorothy (*watching Mary leave*) She doesn't look too good, herself, does she? Worried sick, I shouldn't wonder. I know I would be. (*She turns and notices Barbara*) Barbara? (*More concerned*) Barbara?

Barbara (*snapping out of it*) Sorry. I was just …

Dorothy (*puzzled*) What?

Barbara (*shaking her head*) Nothing.

Dorothy (*amused*) You were miles away.

Barbara (*embarrassed*) Just being stupid. If I'm not careful, I'll be as paranoid as Richard seems to think I am. (*Briskly*) How about a nice glass of something to celebrate your homecoming? (*She heads for the door*)

Dorothy (*frowning*) What do you mean? Paranoid?

Barbara (*pausing*) Well … the cakes and things. The ones I gave the Haighs.

Dorothy What about them?

Barbara (*hesitantly*) I didn't buy them myself. They came from Julia.

Dorothy (*puzzled*) And?

Barbara Well, before I gave them to Allan, I ate a sliver myself. From the fruit slice. The same one he ate later. And shortly after, I was doubled up with pain.

Dorothy (*shocked*) You're not suggesting she did something to it?

Barbara (*helplessly*) I don't know what I'm suggesting. I just … (*Anguished*) Oh, this is ridiculous. I've got to tell someone or I'll go mad. (*Firmly*) But promise you'll not say a word.

Dorothy (*puzzled*) Of course.

Barbara (*returning to sit beside her*) She came round here — on Wednesday afternoon. To bring the cakes. (*She pauses*) But she brought something else, too. Her last will and testament. (*Hastily*) Oh, I know I shouldn't have looked, but I did. It was on the settee and Richard was on the phone. (*Blurting it out*) She's leaving him everything. Millions.

Dorothy gapes in disbelief

He's not said a word to me about it, but I can't stop wondering. Why Richard? Why not one of her precious charities?

Dorothy (*stunned*) Well, I knew she'd been chasing him for years, but … (*Horrified*) You don't think they're having an aff —— (*Firmly*) No, no. Of course they're not. He's got more sense than that, Barbara. Far more sense.

Barbara (*unhappily*) But what if he hasn't? I mean, I know I get on his nerves with constantly being sick. And then there was that Dawson business. It wouldn't surprise me if he had looked elsewhere.

Dorothy (*staunchly*) Well, at least you don't have *him* to worry about any more. Good riddance to bad rubbish.

Barbara (*smiling tightly*) Yes. I think we've seen the last of Mr Dawson. He won't be back here again.

Dorothy And you'll not be attending his funeral, will you?

Barbara (*firmly*) Certainly not. (*Frowning*) Funeral?

Dorothy Well, they won't be having it down here, will they? They'll take him back to where he came from.

Barbara (*blankly*) Who?

Dorothy Eric Dawson.

Barbara looks at her in bewilderment

(*Realizing*) Didn't you know? Has nobody told you?

Barbara (*stunned*) I've been in bed. What happened?

Dorothy Killed on the Link Road, according to Mary. Some time Wednesday night. He was found in a field.

Barbara (*to herself; dully*) After he left here.

Dorothy (*firmly*) Now don't go blaming yourself for that, Barbara. If you ask me, he brought it on himself. Sixty miles an hour's the limit on that road, and he was definitely doing well over that.

Barbara (*rising*) And they're sure it was an accident? It couldn't have been — anything else?

Dorothy (*puzzled*) Such as?

Barbara (*slowly moving* DR) Murder.

Dorothy (*incredulously*) Murder?

Barbara (*almost in a whisper*) He was telling the truth, Dorothy. And I didn't believe him. (*She turns to Dorothy*) Richard is trying to kill me. (*Aghast*) Oh, my God. (*She covers her mouth*)

Dorothy (*concerned*) You don't know what you're saying.

Barbara (*realizing*) It's the money, isn't it? He wants the insurance money.

Dorothy (*rising*) I knew you shouldn't have been on your feet. The minute I saw you. (*Moving towards her*) Let me help you upstairs. You need to lie down.

Barbara You've got to listen to me. He wants me dead. It's the only thing that makes sense. (*Almost gabbling*) I've never been sick in my life — not 'til I came here. And look at me now. For the past few months I've been throwing my insides up and nobody knows why. Who better than a doctor to pump me full of some obscure poison that could finish me off without causing suspicion?

Dorothy (*soothingly*) Let me make you a nice cup of tea.

Barbara (*forcefully*) I don't want any tea. He's been planning it for ages. Since the day we got married. Remember our honeymoon? The boulder that nearly killed me. It was him. He was the one who pushed it.

Dorothy (*shaking her head*) You don't know that.

Barbara When he found out it missed, he had to try again. But not over there. A second accident would have been too much of a coincidence. There could have been suspicions. So we came back here — to sleepy old Bere Knighton — where he could take his time and still carry on with the fancy woman he's been sleeping with for years.

Dorothy I'm sure you're mistaken, Barbara.

Barbara (*tartly*) So why is she leaving him millions in her will? (*Crossing in front of the settee*) If poor Mr Dawson hadn't turned up out of the blue, I'd have been dead before the year was out. And that's why Richard tried to kill him.

Dorothy looks shocked

(*Moving behind the settee*) He had to make sure that Eric couldn't do any more digging in his past and I made the mistake of telling him where to find him. He took my car that night and tried to run him down in Ilfracombe.

Dorothy (*helplessly*) You're letting imagination get the best of you.

Barbara Am I? Then tell me this ——

The telephone rings in the hall

There is a slight pause, then Barbara pulls herself together and exits

Dorothy remains standing

(*Off, into the phone*) Seven–two–five–two–seven. ... Yes. ... I'm sorry. He's not here at present. ... Who? ... I'm sorry? ... I'm afraid I can't. I've no idea. Probably on his rounds by this time. ... Elm Cottage? You mean Elm Cottage in High street? ... I see. Yes. Yes, of course. The minute he gets in.

There is a pause, then Barbara enters, looking shaken

Dorothy looks at her enquiringly

(*Flatly*) The police. They were calling from Elm Cottage. They've just found Julia Moore. At the foot of the stairs.

Dorothy (*shocked*) She's not ... ?

Barbara nods dully

(*Subsiding on to the settee*) Oh, no. I don't believe it.

Barbara (*tonelessly*) It must have happened Wednesday night. She was due to meet friends but never turned up. One of them raised the alarm when they couldn't make contact.

Dorothy (*still reeling from the news*) She must have had a turn with that bug you said was going around. (*She sighs*) Well, I can't say I'd got much time for her, but I never thought she'd end up that way. Grandma Eccles always said the worst accidents happen in the house.

Barbara (*moving around the back of the settee*) Yes. If it really was an accident.

Dorothy (*surprised*) Well, of course it was.

Barbara (*moving to the fireplace*) Was it? (*She turns to Dorothy*) You saw Richard calling on her, Wednesday evening, didn't you? The same night she handed him that will.

Dorothy (*dismayed*) You're not starting that again, are you?

Barbara (*quietly*) We've always had money problems. Right from the beginning. I don't know what he did with it, but we never seemed able to live as we should have done on his salary. But one thing never changed. He always made sure the policies were paid. (*Pointedly*) If I died, he'd be free of debt for years. But the idea of getting millions …

Dorothy (*rising*) I'm sorry, Barbara, but he saved my life and I can't listen to any more of this. Anybody'd think he was Bluebeard, the way you're going on.

Barbara (*quietly*) Maybe he is. Nancy, Grace Walker, Julia Moore. They all loved him and now they're all dead. (*Fiercely*) But he's not getting me. I'll see him in hell, first.

Dorothy (*uneasily*) I'll show myself out. Perhaps you'll feel better if you have a rest?

Barbara (*desperately*) Why won't you believe me?

Dorothy exits

Barbara makes as though to follow then stops, closes her eyes and lets out a deep sigh. A moment later, she subsides on to the settee, lost in thought. The telephone rings again. She does not react and a few moments later, it stops. There is another slight pause

Richard (*off; annoyed*) Barbara? *Barbara?*

Richard enters

Barbara turns her head to look at him

(*Annoyed*) What the hell's happening in Church Walk? The whole damned street's blocked and I'd to detour down The Avenue.

Barbara (*mildly*) Poor old you.

Richard (*fuming*) It's not funny, Barbara. I've a patient at number 17, another in Laurel Close, and I'm running late as it is.

Barbara (*unconcerned*) You'd better be on your way, then, hadn't you?

Richard (*looking at her askance*) Are you all right? Not feeling sick again, are you?

Barbara (*mildly*) No. I didn't touch my tea this morning.

Richard (*puzzled*) Tea?

Barbara (*calmly*) The cup you brought me at half-past seven. It was that you've been putting it in, isn't it? That or the soya milk.

Richard (*irritably*) What the hell are you talking about?

Barbara The poison you've been feeding me for the past twelve months.

Richard What?

Barbara You had it all worked out, didn't you? Get rid of me, collect the insurance money, then a quick dash to the nearest registrar's office with the Merry Widow Moore.

Richard (*in disbelief*) Are you out of your mind? I wouldn't marry Julia if she were the last woman on earth.

Barbara Easy to say. Now you'll never have to.

Richard (*puzzled*) And what's that supposed to mean?

Barbara (*rising*) The police called a few minutes ago. They found her body at the foot of the stairs.

Richard (*stunned*) But — they couldn't have. She's in Norwich, with friends.

Barbara shakes her head

(*Hastily*) I'd better go round. (*He turns to leave*)

Barbara (*harshly*) I wouldn't if I were you. They're not fools, you know. And they're bound to start wondering as soon as they've seen her will.

Richard (*halting*) Will?

Barbara The one that leaves everything to you. Her devoted family doctor. (*She moves towards the fireplace*) Quite a good motive for murder, wouldn't you say?

Richard (*tartly*) Only if you haven't the brains you were born with. (*Curiously*) Who told you? How did you find out?

Barbara Does it matter? (*She turns to him*) The only thing that does, is the fact that she died the day she signed it — and you were seen entering her house only hours before she fell.

Richard (*incredulously*) You're not suggesting I … ? My God. Now I know you're round the bend.

Barbara (*drily*) Better than being dead. (*Moving back to the settee*) I suppose I should feel grateful to her. Leaving everything to you, meant you needn't dispose of me so soon.

Richard (*blustering*) This is ridiculous.

Barbara (*sitting*) Isn't it? Like something from *Midsomer Murders*. Unsuspecting wife finds her husband is a mass murderer and she's next on the list.

Richard (*angrily*) I haven't got time for this. You're as mad as the proverbial hatter.

Barbara (*unconcerned*) I don't think so. The police suspected you of murdering Nancy, Eric Dawson thought you'd killed Grace Walker and I think you murdered Julia. Are you saying we're all wrong?

Richard (*heatedly*) Of course you're bloody wrong. I'd never even heard of Grace Walker 'til he turned up. But he won't be back again, I can tell you. (*Grimly*) I've made quite sure of that.

Barbara (*quietly*) I know. They found his body on Thursday.

Richard looks at her, stunned

Quite a coincidence, wouldn't you say?

Richard (*after a pause*) I need a drink.

Richard goes to the drinks table and pours himself a whisky before turning back to her

Look. There's something you'd better know. (*He moves downstage*) This will business ...

Barbara (*shaking her head*) Don't.

Richard (*tossing the drink back*) It was all her idea. I knew nothing about it 'til she handed it over. There was nothing going on between us, I swear.

Barbara (*uninterested*) Really?

Richard She was in love with me. Had been for years. But it wasn't reciprocated. I'd no more marry her than I'd think of killing you. You have to believe that.

Barbara Oh, I do. (*She smiles*)

Richard (*surprised*) You do?

Barbara Of course. (*She rises*) *You* wouldn't kill anyone — even if your life depended on it.

Richard (*puzzled*) Then what was all that business about?

Barbara (*moving down to the fireplace*) I'd like you to meet someone. An old friend. (*Calling out*) You can come in, now.

The door opens and Eric enters the room

Richard reacts, then turns to Barbara

Richard You said he was dead.

Eric (*reassuringly*) He is. The real Eric Dawson, I mean.

He moves towards Richard, who steps back

I forced him off the road, Wednesday night. Poor sod hadn't a clue what was happening or why I was chasing him. He was dead before the wheels stopped spinning. (*He smiles*) David Young, by the way. (*He holds out his hand*) Barbara's legitimate husband.

Richard stares at him, speechlessly

Barbara You'd better sit down.
Richard (*outraged*) Sit down?
Barbara Not David, Richard. You. Unless you'd prefer to be found on the floor.
Richard (*frowning*) What?
Barbara The whisky. I put something in it.

Richard looks at the glass

There's no antidote. Works perfectly every time.

Eric takes Richard's arm. He attempts to free himself, but Eric presses him on to the settee

You're the fourth, if you're interested. (*She smiles*) Rather amusing, that. The fourth being Dr Forth.
Richard (*attempting to rise*) Get your hands off me.

Eric releases him, but Richard is unable to stand and the glass falls from his hand

Barbara (*easily*) It was David who worked it all out. Find a rich widower, get him to pop the question, then carefully spread the impression that you've never been well since the wedding. A little bit of pressure from a stranger, claiming your beloved may have poisoned his first wife, followed by the death of said stranger, and who'd be surprised if he killed himself through fear of being caught?
Eric (*to Richard*) But you were a real prize. You really had been under suspicion for killing your first wife. Not only that, your little bit on the side had left you millions in her will, and we couldn't pass up a chance to collect that, could we?
Richard (*weakly*) So you killed her.

Eric Just after you left her on Wednesday night. But you don't have to worry. They won't suspect you'd anything to do with it. I left Eric's driving licence halfway down the stairs. They'll find her earrings in his glove box and put two and two together.

Richard (*faintly*) Who was he?

Eric Exactly who I said he was. A computer salesman from Buxton. I chatted him up in the hotel, found out his itinerary, then arranged his little "accident". And while we're on the subject — Grace Walker is in Dover Cemetery. Died of pneumonia, sixty years ago. Useful little lady. We drink to her memory, every time we wrap up a scam.

Richard's eyes close and his head lolls. Eric stoops over him and lifts one of his eyelids

I think he's gone. (*He straightens himself*)

Barbara (*coldly*) We'll give it a few more minutes. Get working on the note. "Can't live without her. Were going to be married as soon as my divorce came through, et cetera." And let me check it over before you seal the envelope.

Eric (*moving to the desk*) Let's hope my forging skills haven't deserted me. (*He sits and prepares himself*)

Barbara They haven't up to now. (*She crosses to the drinks table and picks up the whisky bottle*) I'll get rid of this and bring a fresh one.

Eric (*hastily*) Not fresh. We need the fingerprints. Wash it out and refill. About a third. Tip the rest down the sink and get rid of the bottle. (*He begins to write carefully*)

Barbara What about the crystals? Do we leave them on the settee?

Eric (*impatiently*) Wherever. Next to the bottle if you like. Let me get this right. (*He continues to write*)

Barbara (*glancing at Richard's body*) Who's going to find him? Me? Or one of the others?

Eric (*still writing*) Best if you do it. Who else'd have a key? Go do some shopping and find him when you get back.

Barbara (*thoughtfully*) I could drive to the hospital and see Allan Haigh. (*Wryly*) I quite liked him, and feel a bit guilty for putting him there. But it added to suspicions that Richard was poisoning me, so that seed's firmly planted now. I could even bring Mary back with me. If we came in together …

Eric Good idea. You can give me a call when the police have gone.

Barbara Where are you going?

Eric Down to South Molton. I'll keep the mobile on 'til we've fixed up where to meet, then dump it. Even if they have suspicions, they'll never be able to connect us. Better take yours, too. No sense in being careless. (*Ruefully*) Should have 'em gold plated, really. Money they've earned us.

Barbara (*heading for the door*) I'll bring it through.

The door opens and Dorothy appears

Dorothy (*quietly*) I wouldn't bother, if I were you.

Eric looks round, startled. Barbara reacts

Barbara What are you doing here?

Dorothy I never left. When I got into the hall, I remembered the pot of honey I brought round for you, and went into the kitchen to leave it there. I was just coming out again when Richard arrived. I didn't want to be in the middle of a family row, so I hid behind the door 'til he came in here. I could hear what went on, but just as I was creeping down the hall, I saw the front door opening again, and shot back into the kitchen. Then he came in. (*Indicating Eric with her head*) A dead man. A man who'd been killed on the Link Road — and I watched him listening outside this door.

Eric (*rising and grabbing her arm*) You nosy old bitch.

Dorothy (*struggling to free herself*) You're hurting.

Eric (*menacingly*) Not half as much as I'm going to.

Dorothy (*defiantly*) Oh, no you're not. Not by a long chalk. You'll not be hurting anyone again. I heard it all, you see? Heard everything. And you're going to pay for it.

Barbara (*smoothly*) Is that so? Going to tell the police, are you? Going to set the law on us? I don't think so, Dorothy. I somehow don't think so.

Eric Another body's not going to worry us. We've had lots of practice. And you know what they say? Practice makes perfect.

Dorothy (*defiantly*) You won't lay a finger on me.

Barbara And why not, I wonder?

Dorothy (*harshly*) Because I've already told the police. They'll be here any minute.

There is a slight pause as they react

Eric (*smiling*) Naughty, naughty. Mustn't tell fibs, Mrs L. If you've been listening at the keyhole, how could you call the police? The phone's outside the door. Do you think we'd not have heard you?

Dorothy (*spitefully*) You might have done if I'd used it. That's why I used hers. (*Indicating Barbara*) The one she keeps in the kitchen.

There is a stunned silence

Barbara (*scornfully*) She's lying.
Dorothy Am I?

The door chimes sound

Then what's that?

Barbara and Eric stand frozen

Male voice (*off*) Police. Could you open the door, Mrs Forth?

Dorothy smiles coldly as Barbara and Eric look at each other in dismay

Will you open the door, please?

The Lights fade to Black-out

CURTAIN

FURNITURE AND PROPERTY LIST

ACT I
SCENE 1

On stage: French windows with rich drapes (open at start)
Paved patio with a garden view. *On it*: floral tubs
Large, glass-fronted bookcase. *In it*: hardcover books
Open-fronted bookcase. *In it*: paperback books
Drinks table. *On it*: assorted glasses, various spirits including whisky
Adam-style fireplace with mantel. *On it*: assorted ornaments, two large oriental vases, clock. Above it: mirror
Two tall recessed windows (open at start) overlooking mature trees, with drapes and deep ledges. *On ledges*: bowls of fresh flowers
Built-in unit. *In it*: music centre, speakers, records, CDs
Built-in unit. *In it*: TV, VCR, video tapes
Half-round table. *On it*: attractive modern lamp
Writing desk. *On it*: writing paper, envelopes, pens, framed photographs, medical books, dusters, spray polish cans, etc.
Ladder-back chair
Settee. *On it*: cushions. *On one arm*: rubber gloves
Occasional table
Easy chair. *On it*: cushions
Thickly carpeted floor
Decorative plates and pictures
Window cleaners
Vacuum cleaner
Light switch L of the door
Shaggy rug (for **Dorothy**)

Off stage: Two mugs of coffee (**Barbara**)
Leather bowls bag (**Allan**)
Handbag (**Mary**)
Slim attaché case (**Richard**)
Handbag (**Julia**)

Personal: **Barbara**; purse, ten pound note, business card

SCENE 2

Re-set: Any books back on shelves
            Windows closed
            Check curtains open

Set: Sheaffer pen and **Julia**'s handbag containing compact and lipstick
            on desk

Off stage: Jacket, **Julia**'s coat (**Richard**)
            Shopping bags (**Dorothy**)
            Desk diary (**Barbara**)
            Tray containing four teacups and saucers, teapot, sugar bowl, two
            small milk jugs, three teaspoons, small plate of assorted biscuits
            (**Barbara**)

Personal: **Julia**: glass of brandy
            Richard: tumbler of whisky
            Barbara: hanky

ACT II
SCENE 1

Re-set: Curtains open, general tidy up

Strike: Tray containing sugar bowl, milk jug and plate. Cups, saucers,
            spoons

Off stage: Cake box tied with pink ribbon containing two slices of cake,
            handbag containing long, slim envelope (**Julia**)
            Medical case (**Richard**)

Personal: **Barbara**: wristwatch

SCENE 2

Strike: Cake box and medical case

Off stage: Small suitcase (**Mary**)

Personal: **Dorothy**: small jar of honey in pocket

LIGHTING PLOT

Practical fittings required: table lamp, electric fire

ACT I
Scene 1

To open: *Daytime interior lighting*

Cue 1   **Barbara** and **Dorothy** look silently at each other.   (Page 19)
               Fade to Black-out

Scene 2

To open: *Evening interior lighting; practicals on*

Cue 2   **Richard** enters and crosses to the women   (Page 36)
               Fade to Black-out

ACT II
Scene 1

To open: *Daytime interior lighting; electric fire on low*

Cue 3   **Barbara** turns up electric fire   (Page 40)
               Increase glow from fire

Cue 4   **Allan** stands motionless as the outside door slams   (Page 52)
               Fade to Black-out

Scene 2

To open: *Daytime interior lighting*

Cue 5   **Male Voice**: "Will you open the door, please?"   (Page 68)
               Fade to Black-out

EFFECTS PLOT

ACT I

Cue 1   **Barbara**: " ... I'm sorting them out, you can —"   (Page 3)
Doorbell chimes

Cue 2   **Allan**: "Well, if you happen to change your minds ..."   (Page 6)
Doorbell chimes

Cue 3   **Dorothy**: "Well, far be it from *me* to criticize."   (Page 12)
Doorbell chimes

Cue 4   **Barbara**: "I'll get the tea."   (Page 28)
Doorbell chimes

Cue 5   **Barbara**: "I wasn't thinking. Anyone like a biscuit?" (Page 34)
Doorbell chimes

ACT II

Cue 6   To open   (Page 37)
Light classical music plays softly from music centre;
* after a pause doorbell chimes*

Cue 7   **Richard** crosses to the music centre to turn it off   (Page 37)
Classical music stops

Cue 8   **Richard**: (*softly*) "Millions."   (Page 40)
The telephone rings in the hall

Cue 9   **Barbara**: "You look like you've swallowed a wasp." (Page 42)
Doorbell chimes

Cue 10   **Richard**: "... changes her mind and gobbles the rest." (Page 45)
The telephone rings in the hall

Cue 11   **Richard** exits   (Page 46)
            The outside door slams

Cue 12   **Barbara**: "They'll cheer Mary up no end."   (Page 46)
            Doorbell chimes

Cue 13   **Eric** and **Barbara** exit. There is a pause   (Page 51)
            The front door closes firmly

Cue 14   **Allan** searches through various papers on the desk   (Page 52)
            The front door slams shut

Cue 15   **Richard** exits and **Allan** stands motionless   (Page 52)
            The outside door slams

Cue 16   When ready   (Page 53)
            Doorbell chimes; pause; doorbell chimes

Cue 17   **Dorothy** looks at a small jar of honey and sighs   (Page 55)
            Doorbell chimes

Cue 18   **Barbara**: "Am I? Then tell me this —"   (Page 61)
            The telephone rings

Cue 19   **Barbara** subsides on to the settee, lost in thought   (Page 62)
            The telephone rings

Cue 20   **Dorothy**: "Am I?"   (Page 68)
            The front doorbell chimes